PERSPECTIVES

2000

ABE/ESL
Ses. '91

PERSPECTIVES

2000

Intermediate
English 1

- **ANNA UHL CHAMOT**
- **ISOBEL RAINEY DE DIAZ**
- **JOAN BAKER DE GONZALEZ**
- **LINDA LEE**
- **RICHARD YORKEY**

Heinle & Heinle Publishers
A Division of Wadsworth, Inc.
Boston, Massachusetts 02116

HH

Publisher: Stanley J. Galek
Editorial Director: Christopher Foley
Assistant Editor: Erik Gundersen
Project Coordinator: Talbot F. Hamlin

Production Supervisor: Patricia Jalbert
Manufacturing Coordinator: Lisa McLaughlin
Text Designer: Jean Hammond
Cover Designer: The Graphics Studio/Gerry Rosentswieg
Illustrator: Joseph Veno Studio

Acknowledgments

The authors and publisher would like to acknowledge the contributions of the following individuals who reviewed the Perspectives 2000 program at various stages of development and who offered many insights and suggestions:

- Mary J. Erickson
  University of Texas, Pan American
- Barbara Ann Jaffe
  Santa Monica College &
  West Los Angeles College
- Peggy Kazkaz
  William Rainey Harper College
- Big-Qu Chin Seeto
  City College of San Francisco

- Lúcia Alves de Aragão, Rosa Erlichman, Sonia Godoy, and Maria Inês Lopes
  União Cultural, São Paulo, Brazil
- Ryland Moore
  University of Hawaii at Manoa
- Alexandre Oliveira
  Casa Thomas Jefferson, Brasília, Brazil
- Robert L. Saitz
  Boston University

Text and photo credits are on page 180

Heinle & Heinle Publishers is a division of Wadsworth, Inc.

Manufactured in the United States of America

ISBN 0-8384-2003-6

10 9 8 7 6 5 4 3 2 1

Contents

COMMUNICATION   **GRAMMAR**   **SKILLS**

Talking about daily routines •
Comparing things •
Requesting help

Present and present continuous
tenses • Past and past
continuous tenses • Time
words: *when, while, whenever, as
soon as, once* • Comparatives,
superlatives

Analyzing a graph • Predicting •
Making comparisons • Evaluating •
Using context clues • Following a
sequence • Using visual images •
Listening for specific information

Describing past activities •
Asking/answering questions about
appointments, schedules •
Interviewing • Asking/answering
personal questions • Talking
about changes over time

Present perfect tenses •
Indefinite time expressions: *ever,
never, recently, just* • Indefinite
time expressions: *already, yet* •
Present perfect continuous
tense • Present tense (Review)

Predicting • Using context clues •
Interpreting a chart • Reading a
schedule • Making comparisons •
Reading a census form • Problem
solving • Planning a questionnaire • Organizational planning

Discussing fashion and fads •
Asking/answering questions about
attitudes, abilities •
Interviewing • Asking/answering
probing questions • Explaining
choices, preferences • Expressing
surprise

Gerunds • Infinitives •
Verbs followed by infinitives and
gerunds • Present perfect tense
(Review)

Using context clues •
Restating • Summarizing • Using
visual images • Supporting an
opinion • Inferencing • Drawing
conclusions

Using analogies • Discussing pros
and cons of possible future
actions • Suggesting alternative
explanations and solutions •
Discussing problem solving

Future possible conditional
statements • Modals to express
possibility: *may, might, could,
can* • Verb tenses (Review)

Identifying the main idea • Using
context clues • Inferencing •
Problem solving • Interpreting
quotes • Restating

Introduction

PERSPECTIVES 2000 is a two-level course for ESL and EFL learners at the intermediate and upper-intermediate levels. It may be used following Heinle & Heinle's INTERCOM 2000 or any other introductory ESL/EFL series.

PERSPECTIVES 2000's holistic approach to language learning integrates speaking, listening, reading, and writing activities by organizing them around compelling contemporary themes. The series is developed from a tri-dimensional syllabus integrating communicative, grammatical, and critical thinking objectives. These objectives are interwoven throughout the four language skills.

PERSPECTIVES 2000 also uses a "spiraled" approach to learning which provides extensive review, reinforcement, and expansion. This approach promotes the gradual and secure development of listening, reading, and writing skills.

Each level of PERSPECTIVES 2000 includes the following components:

- Student text
- Workbook
- Teacher's edition
- Tape program

A separate Testing Program provides assessment and evaluation instruments for both levels.

FEATURES OF PERSPECTIVES 2000

PERSPECTIVES 2000 incorporates a range of features designed to maximize its usefulness as an instructional tool and to make it attractive and easy to use by students and instructors alike. These features include:

- clearly-listed objectives at the beginning of each unit
- all-new readings with built-in student appeal
- comprehension and discussion questions that focus on building reading and critical thinking skills

- an integrated grammar program with carefully-sequenced structures introduced in readings, explained in clear, easy-to-read charts, practiced in a variety of exercises, and periodically reviewed
- expanded exercises and activities to provide extensive practice in all four skill areas
- entirely new art program and design
- workbook exercises directly correlated to student text
- complete tape program including all readings, comprehension/discussion questions, pronunciation exercises, and listening activities

THE RATIONALE

Communicative competence is the primary goal of the PERSPECTIVES 2000 course. To achieve this, the series provides interesting, adult-oriented content around which the exercises and activities have been written. As students read, write, speak, and listen, they both learn content and practice important skills in all four basic language areas.

PERSPECTIVES 2000's holistic approach provides students with the opportunity to practice language in natural and interesting contexts, using the processes of listening, speaking, reading, and writing. Activities built around each topic include dialogues, role plays, group discussions, and process writing assignments.

Because students at this level generally want the support of explicit grammar, the text provides concise grammatical explanations and examples in easy-to-read charts. Students are then given the opportunity to use grammatical structures in activities that progress from controlled to open-ended.

ORGANIZATION OF THE TEXT

Each of the two books in the PERSPECTIVES 2000 course has nine units. The first two units in Level One are review units. A thorough review of verb tenses and structures such as comparatives and superlatives enables teachers to evaluate their students' level of proficiency as they begin this course.

Each of the nine units includes the following features:

Unit Opener. The unit begins with a page of photographs, drawings, or charts accompanied by thought-provoking discussion questions. The purpose of the *Unit Opener* is to prepare students for the information in the unit by getting them to relate the unit topic to their own experiences, thus building on their cognitive frameworks.

Reading. Each unit has two reading passages — one immediately following the *Unit Opener* and one at the end of the unit. The two readings deal with different aspects of the same topic. At the same time, the readings have been designed to use specific grammar structures in a natural context.

Following each reading is a series of discussion questions that ask students to use a variety of skills ranging from basic recall and literal comprehension to higher-level thinking skills that require students to evaluate ideas, analyze information, and make inferences.

Vocabulary in Context. These activities help students to develop the skill of using context clues to determine the meaning of lexical items which appear in the reading.

Focus on Grammar. Each new or review structure is presented in an easy-to-read reference chart providing concise rules and numerous examples. When the grammar chart reviews a structure already taught in the book, the title *Remember* is used.

Practice. These exercises provide practice in using the structures presented in *Focus on Grammar*. The purpose of these exercises is to allow students to use the new structures in a controlled situation until the structures are clearly understood. When students are comfortable with the pattern, they can then use it to express their own ideas. As soon as this is apparent, students move on to the *Interact* phase.

Interact. *Interact* exercises move beyond the controlled production of the *Practice* exercises. Students now use the featured structure in short dialogues built around a variety of interpersonal situations. During the culminating phase of this exercise, students negotiate situations which focus on their own needs, interests, and experiences. The *Interact* exercises are designed specifically for use in pairs or groups of three.

Listening. A wide variety of *Listening* activities are provided, all designed to help students strengthen their auditory comprehension skills, both literal and inferential. The varied formats and content of the *Listening* exercises provide experience in understanding oral communication in many contexts. (Additional listening practice is provided through the Tape Program which includes recordings of not only the listening exercises, but also of all readings, comprehension/discussion questions, and pronunciation examples.)

Writing. *Writing* assignments are always built around the theme of the unit. They incorporate many aspects of process writing, including peer evaluation before production of a final draft.

Pronunciation. Short exercises focus on particular phonological characteristics of English, with contrast of typically confusing sounds.

Get Together. These communicative activities give students the opportunity to synthesize what they have learned in the section or unit. Students are asked to talk together about subjects that are sometimes serious, sometimes humorous. In this section, student conversation is free of constraint; students are expected to express their own ideas and opinions. Through completing the cooperative tasks in the *Get Togethers*, students work on developing the art of conversation in English.

Vocabulary Lists. A selected list of words and expressions appears at the end of each unit. These include new, interesting, and specialized words and expressions used in the exercises and activities. Some of these items are new forms of known words.

Identifying Unit Components. The units are divided into numbered sections and lettered activities within these sections. Numbered sections in all units include *Reading*, *Focus on Grammar*, *Listening*, *Writing*, *Pronunciation*, and *Get Together*. The lettered exercises and activities provide practice and application of the subjects in the numbered sections.

ANCILLARY COMPONENTS

Teacher's Edition. The *Teacher's Editions* contain the full text of the student book together with teaching suggestions for each page, scripts and suggested answers for all *Listening* activities, and suggested correct answers for exercises in the text and workbook.

Workbook. The *Workbooks* contain a variety of written exercises to provide additional practice and application for material taught in the student text. Most *Workbook* exercises are suggested for use after specific numbered text sections; others combine a variety of skills taught in the unit and can best be used after the unit has been completed.

Tape Program. The tapes provide a model for students and also contain the *Listening* exercises. The cassettes may be used in the classroom, the laboratory, or at home.

Testing Program. Tests assess and evaluate student performance and measure achievement of the goals of each unit and of the program as a whole.

COMMUNICATION
Talking about daily routines ▪
Comparing things ▪ Requesting help

GRAMMAR
Present and present continuous tenses ▪
Past and past continuous tenses ▪ Time
words: *when, while, whenever, as soon
as, once* ▪ Comparatives, superlatives

Asleep and Awake

How do you feel when you wake up in the morning? People who like to get up early in the morning are called "larks." People who like to stay up late at night are called "owls." Are you a "lark" or an "owl"? Why do you think some people are "larks" and others are "owls"?

The chart at the right shows how a person's body temperature changes during the day. When is body temperature at its highest? Lowest? The dotted line shows how alert, or awake, the person feels during the day. Is there any relationship between alertness and body temperature?

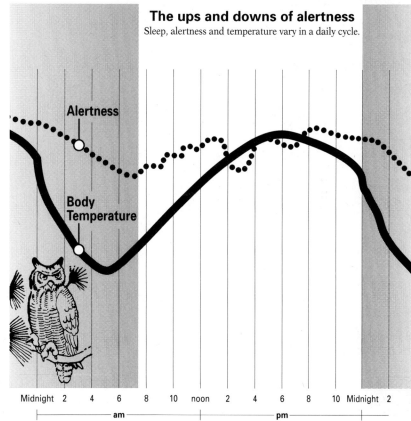

The ups and downs of alertness
Sleep, alertness and temperature vary in a daily cycle.

Alertness

Body Temperature

Midnight 2 4 6 8 10 noon 2 4 6 8 10 Midnight 2

am ——————— pm ———————

Listening to your body rhythms

Time for a Nap?

Like many creative geniuses, the Italian painter Leonardo Da Vinci was a workaholic. There were days when he just didn't want to waste time sleeping. To get the rest he needed, Da Vinci came up with an interesting solution: he took a fifteen minute nap, six times a day. This means that in a twenty-four hour period, he got a total of an hour and a half of sleep. This schedule might not work for everyone, but it does make you wonder how much sleep a person really needs.

Body Rhythms

Researchers in a new field of science called chronobiology are studying the body's natural rhythms, or patterns, to find out just what makes people sleepy. Chronobiologists have learned that a person's temperature, blood pressure, and hormone levels go up and down in a regular pattern that repeats itself every twenty-four hours. During the day, a person's blood pressure rises by as much as twenty percent. Body temperature varies daily by as much as two degrees.

The daily cycle of body temperature affects how a person feels at different times during the day. For most people, body temperature begins to drop in the early evening. This slows other bodily functions and makes you feel drowsy. Around daybreak, body temperature rises and you begin to feel more alert.

Larks and Owls

The ups and downs of your body temperature determine whether you will be a "lark" or an "owl." A lark's body temperature rises sharply in the morning, reaching a peak between late afternoon and early evening. This is when larks are the most productive. But as body temperature decreases, so does energy level. By nine o'clock, larks are getting sleepy. Owls work on a different schedule. Their body temperature rises more gradually and peaks later in the day. This allows them to keep going while larks are getting ready for bed.

During World War II, British Prime Minister Winston Churchill scheduled meetings around his naps. He thought naps helped to keep him alert.

Albert Einstein took regular naps to refresh his mind.

New Findings

Many chronobiologists now think that the time of day a person gets drug treatment for cancer affects the success of treatment. Other studies are revealing that we do different types of work better at different times of the day. Physical coordination, for example, peaks during the afternoon. This is the best time of day to do work with your hands such as typing or carpentry. And some studies show that eight to nine hours of sleep every night might not be necessary. Frequent naps might work just as well or even better. Findings such as these are helping people to organize their lives so that they work with their natural rhythms rather than against them.

Thomas Edison, the inventor of the light bulb, thought sleeping all night wasted a lot of time. Taking naps wasted less time.

A | **Comprehension and Discussion**

1. What happens to a person's body temperature during the day?
2. How are "owls" and "larks" different?
3. What advice will a chronobiologist give to a doctor who uses drug treatment?
4. What do you do when you feel drowsy in the afternoon?
5. When do you feel the most energetic? Why do you think this is so?
6. Do you think chronobiology is a useful field of study? Why or why not?

B Vocabulary in Context

Find the word or phrase that best completes the sentence. Write the letter of the correct answer.

1. Albert Einstein often *took a nap* when he felt sleepy in the afternoon. When you *take a nap*, you _____.
   a. rest without sleeping
   b. sleep for a short time
   c. eat a little

2. When you feel *drowsy* in the middle of the afternoon, it is difficult to think. When you feel *drowsy*, you feel _____.
   a. hungry
   b. sad
   c. sleepy

3. Most *workaholics* don't sleep very much. They think sleeping is a waste of time. A *workaholic* is a person who _____.
   a. can't sleep
   b. wants to sleep all the time
   c. wants to work all the time

4. A "lark's" body temperature rises *sharply* in the morning. When temperature rises *sharply*, it _____.
   a. stays the same
   b. rises quickly
   c. rises slowly

5. An "owl's" body temperature rises *gradually*. A *gradual* rise is a _____ rise.
   a. quick
   b. repeated
   c. slow

6. The rain here certainly *affects* how I feel. It makes me feel sad. When something *affects* you, it _____.
   a. causes a change in you
   b. makes you feel tired
   c. makes you unhappy

7. Coffee makes some people feel more *alert*. When you feel *alert*, you feel _____.
   a. tired
   b. sad
   c. responsive

8. The temperature outside yesterday *peaked* at 80 degrees F. When something *peaks*, it _____.
   a. reaches a high point
   b. reaches a low point
   c. stays the same

9. A person's body temperature *varies* during the day.
When something *varies*, it _____.
a. stays the same
b. changes
c. increases

10. The music had a strong *rhythm*.
A *rhythm* is _____.
a. a regular repeated pattern
b. a very loud sound
c. an irregular change

2 Focus on Grammar

Simple Present and Present Continuous Tenses
is (are) + verb - ing

Rule	Example
1. Use the simple present tense to talk about things that happen regularly or habitually.	a. I usually **get up** before 7 a.m. b. He **doesn't like** to go to bed early. c. **Do** you usually **feel** energetic in the morning?
2. You can also use the simple present to talk about things that are generally true— scientific facts, for example.	a. A person's body temperature **varies** during the day. b. Blood pressure **rises** by as much as 20 percent over a twenty-four hour period.
3. Use the present continuous tense to describe something that is happening now or temporarily.	a. Nate **is** still **sleeping** so we can't leave yet. b. Research **is** now **providing** new information about body rhythms. c. I'**m** not **taking** a course this semester.

A Practice

Fill in the blanks with the correct form of the verbs.

1. The peak time of alertness for most people (be) _____*is*_____ the late morning. Creative people usually (do) _____ their best work at this time of day. This (be) _____ also the best time of day to do math problems or to write difficult letters.

2. The senses— sight, hearing, taste, smell, and touch— (be) _____ at their best in the late afternoon and early evening. Is this why many people (like) _____ good food and candlelight at the end of the day?

3. A person (do) _____ best in sports in the late afternoon and early evening. Physical coordination (be) _____ at a peak at this time of day. Swimmers and runners (perform) _____ better in the evening than in the morning.
4. Think about what you (do) _____ right now. If you (type) _____ or doing something else with your hands, are you doing a good job? If you (make) _____ a lot of mistakes, you should probably stop and rest for a while.

B | Interact

Work with a partner. Find out when he or she:

> *Example:* usually eats breakfast
>
> A: When do you usually eat breakfast?
>
> B: Hm. I usually eat breakfast around 8.

1. usually gets up
2. usually goes to bed
3. usually studies
4. usually gets exercise
5. feels very energetic during the day
6. feels very alert during the day
7. feels physically tired during the day
8. begins to feel sleepy in the evening
9. finds it difficult to think or work
10. wants to sleep during the day
11. is ready to begin studying in the morning
12. _____

C | Practice

Make two lists about your daily routine. On one list write three positive things. On the other list, write three negative things. For example:

Positive things about my daily routine:

I don't have to get up early in the morning.

I have time for a long relaxing breakfast.

I get lots of exercise.

Negative things about my daily routine:

I spend a lot of time traveling to work.

Usually I don't have time to eat lunch.

I get home late in the evening.

D | Get Together

Look carefully at this picture for one minute. Study all the things that are happening. Then close your book and write down everything you can remember about the picture. Use the present continuous tense in your sentences. Then, compare your answers with another student's answers.

Study the cartoon by Rube Goldberg. Then fill in the blanks with the correct form of the verb in parentheses.

When the sun (come up) _____comes up_____ in the morning, the magnifying glass (burn) _____ a hole in the bag. As soon as there (be) _____ a hole in the bag, water drips down into the ladle, or big spoon. The water (push) _____ one end of the ladle down while the other end (rise) _____ and lifts up a gate. This (allow) _____ a heavy ball to roll down the chute. A rope then (lift) _____ the bed into a vertical position and the sleeper drops into his shoes.

P.S. You can't go back and sneak a few winks because there's no place to lie down!

RUBE GOLDBERG

3 Focus on Grammar

Simple Past and Past Continuous
was (were) + verb -ing

Rule	Example
1. Use the simple past tense to describe an activity that began and ended at a definite time in the past.	a. I **got up** at 6 a.m. b. He **worked** from 8 a.m. until 6 p.m. c. When I was a child, I usually **played** with my sister. d. She **lived** in Puerto Rico from 1990 to 1991.
2. Use the past continuous tense to show that a temporary action was taking place at the same time as another event or point in time in the past.	a. I **was getting up** when the door bell rang. b. They arrived while he **was working** outdoors. c. I **was playing** with my sister when she fell down. d. She **was living** in Puerto Rico when she met him.
3. In some cases, either the simple past or the past continuous can be used. In these cases, the past continuous gives more emphasis to the ongoing nature of the event or situation.	a. The clocks **weren't working** all day yesterday. b. The clocks **didn't work** all day yesterday. c. She **was living** in Paris during the war. d. She **lived** in Paris during the war. e. While I **was working** there, I was also going to school. f. While I **worked** there, I also went to school.

A Practice

Fill in the blanks with the correct tense and form of the verbs in parentheses. In some cases, more than one answer may be correct.

Gabriel Garcia Marquez

When the writer Gabriel Garcia Marquez began writing full-time, he (work) ____worked____ from nine in the morning until two in the afternoon, when his children returned from school. He tried to work in the afternoon while his children (play) _____ outside, but nothing he (write) _____ at this time of day was any good. He usually (have) _____to throw away his afternoon's work. That's when he decided to do other things in the afternoon, such as meeting people and giving interviews.

Jack London

The writer Jack London wrote 20 hours a day, or so he claimed. Before he (go) _____ to sleep, he set his alarm clock to go off four hours later. He usually (sleep) _____ heavily, so he didn't hear the noise when the alarm went off. Because he often (not/hear) _____ the alarm clock, he set up a system to drop a weight on his head when the alarm (go off) _____.

Wallace Stevens

The poet Wallace Stevens (work) _____ as a lawyer in New York when he met the president of an insurance company in Connecticut. The president of the company offered him a job and in 1916, Stevens moved to Hartford, Connecticut. Stevens had a productive work schedule while he (live) _____ in Hartford. He usually (get up) _____ at six in the morning and read for two hours. Then he (walk) _____ three miles to his office at the insurance company. At noon, he (go) _____ for another walk instead of eating lunch. While he (walk) _____, he thought about his poetry. At the end of the day, he (walk) _____ home— another hour's walk. But he still wasn't ready to rest. After dinner, he (work) _____ on his poetry until he went to bed at 9 p.m.

Carlos Fuentes says that he is a morning writer. By eight-thirty in the morning he (be) _____ usually at his desk and working. He usually stops working at twelve-thirty and (go) _____ for a swim. After lunch he reads and takes a walk. While he (walk) _____, he plans his writing for the next day.

B Practice

Fill in the blanks with the correct tense and form of the berbs in parentheses.

1. (do) He _____did_____ poorly on the test because he was so tired.
2. (be) Some people _____ more alert in the afternoon.
3. (rise) The body temperature of "larks" _____ sharply in the morning.
4. (sleep) He came into the room while I _____.
5. (feel) I _____ pretty good when I got up this morning.
6. (show) Some research _____ that body rhythms affect medical treatment.
7. (peak) Body temperature usually _____ in the late afternoon.
8. (be) Chronobiology _____ the study of the body's natural rhythmic patterns.
9. (cook) The accident happened while he _____ breakfast.
10. (begin) Interest in chronobiology _____ in the 1940s.
11. (go) Body temperature _____ up and down over a twenty-four hour period.
12. (finish) In 1979, there was an accident at the Three Mile Island nuclear power plant in the United States. The disaster occurred when tired employees _____ work.

C Interact

Ask your classmates questions to find someone who fits each of the descriptions below. Write down the name of the classmate who fits the description. Find someone in your class who:

1. was born in a city
2. was born in a small town
3. was born in another country
4. didn't like school when he or she was a child
5. grew up in a large family
6. studied a foreign language in high school
7. lives with a relative
8. has a birthday the same month as yours

Read these letters from the newspaper column "Advice from Marla." Circle the verbs in the present tense. Underline the verbs in the past tense. Then, write Marla's response to the second letter.

Dear Marla:
I read your letter about morning people and night people in yesterday's newspaper. You called them 'larks' and 'owls.' You said, "Larks and owls have different body rhythms." Well, I think that's crazy. I think owls are just lazy people. My parents were 'owls.' They always slept late in the morning, and their kids always had to make their own breakfast. I don't think that's right. People should get up with the sun!
                                    A Lark in Pasadena

Dear Lark:
I am an 'owl.' I sleep late in the morning, but I am not a lazy person. Like most people, I get 7 hours of sleep every twenty-four hours. I also work many hours— usually at night. When my children were young, I did get up to make their breakfast. I hated getting up early, but I did it. Now my daughter is forty years old, and she is quite capable of making her own breakfast. Of course there are times when it is necessary to get up early. But there are also times when we can follow a routine that best fits our own body rhythms.
                                    Marla

Dear Marla:
Can you read another owl vs. lark letter? I hope so. My husband says that I am lazy because I don't get up full of energy at 6:30 a.m. The worst noise in the world to me is the alarm clock in the morning. I get up when it rings, but I always feel terrible. I never feel really good until noon. Do you have any suggestions?
                                    Louise in San Diego

Now write Marla's answer to Louise.

4 Focus on Grammar

Time Words
when, while, whenever, as soon as, once

Rule	Example
1. when Use *when* + a verb in the simple past tense to describe an activity that took place at a specific moment in the past.	a. **When** the phone rang, he jumped out of his chair and answered it. b. **When** I arrived, no one was there. c. **When** I came into the room, he was taking a nap. d. Were you working **when** I called?

(continued)

Time Words
(continued)

Rule

2. while

Use *while* + the past continuous tense to connect two ongoing activities taking place at the same time.
Use *while* to show an ongoing activity that is interrupted by a sudden event.

Example

a. They were making a lot of noise **while** the other children were trying to study.
b. **While** they were living in England, their children were going to school in the United States.
c. The car broke down **while** I was driving home.
d. The rain started **while** we were walking home.

3. whenever

Whenever means "at any time that."

a. **Whenever** she gets sleepy, she stops driving.
b. I can come over **whenever** you need me.

4. as soon as, once

As soon as and *once* mean "immediately after." *As soon as* has a greater sense of urgency than *once*.

a. I jumped out of bed **as soon as** I woke up.
b. **Once** I heard the alarm clock, I jumped out of bed.
c. **As soon as** she saw the fire, she called for help.

A Practice

Complete the following sentences.

1. I will call you as soon as I _check into the hotel (or get home, etc.)_.
2. He stopped driving as soon as he _____.
3. I was listening to music while she _____.
4. I got drowsy when _____.
5. I made a lot of mistakes while I _____.
6. Whenever I _____, I feel terrible the next day.
7. While I _____, she fell asleep.
8. He wrote the story while he was _____.
9. I didn't want to disturb her while she was _____.
10. Everyone left the room when _____.

5 Focus on Grammar

Comparative and Superlative Forms of Adjectives
-er, -est

Rule	Example		
	Simple	Comparative	Superlative
1. For most one-syllable adjectives: add *-er* for the comparative form; add *-est* for the superlative form.	tall short long	taller (than) shorter longer	(the) tallest shortest longest
2. For most two-syllable adjectives: use *more* for the comparative form; use *most* for the superlative form.	alert famous	more alert more famous	most alert most famous
3. For two-syllable adjectives ending in *-y:* change the *-y* to *-i* and add *-er* and *-est.*	busy happy	busier happier	busiest happiest
4. These two-syllable adjectives can take either -er/-est or more/most: *angry, clever, friendly, gentle, handsome, narrow, quiet, simple.*	friendly	friendlier more friendly	friendliest most friendly
5. For adjectives with three or more syllables: use *more* for the comparative; use *most* for the superlative	energetic	more energetic	most energetic
6. Some adjectives have irregular forms in the comparative and superlative.	good bad	better worse	best worst

tall   taller   tallest

A Practice

Fill in each blank with the correct form of one of the words below. In some cases more than one answer may be correct.

bad   good

I can't understand why my grades are getting ___worse___. I stay up late every night to study, but my grades aren't getting _____. Last night I studied until three in the morning, but the grade I got on today's test was the _____ grade yet. If I don't get a _____ grade on the next test, I'll be in trouble. I would like to know how An always gets _____ grades. He went to bed early last night, and then this morning he just took a little time to look over his notes before the test. He got the _____ grade in the class. What am I doing wrong?

B Interact

With a partner, make up untrue statements, as in the example. Then disagree with the statement.

A: <u>Bikes cost more than cars.</u>
B: That's ridiculous! <u>Bikes don't cost more than cars. They are much less expensive than cars.</u>

A: <u>Belgium is bigger than France.</u>
B: That's ridiculous! <u>Belgium isn't bigger than France. It's smaller than France.</u>

A: _____.
B: That's ridiculous! _____.

1. swimming/scuba diving
2. an apple/a candy bar
3. a computer/a pen
4. Puerto Rico/Iceland
5. Mexico/Canada
6. motorcycle/bicycle
7. presidents/vice presidents
8. newspapers/magazines
9. a Porsche/a Honda
10. _____

With a partner, practice this dialogue.

A: Do you feel <u>more energetic</u> in the morning or in the afternoon?
B: Gee, I don't know. I think I usually feel <u>more energetic</u> in the <u>morning</u>.

A: Great! I need to <u>move my piano</u> tomorrow <u>morning</u>. Can you help?
B: I've been had!

A: Do you feel _____ in the morning or in the afternoon?
B: Gee, I don't know. I think I usually feel _____ in the _____.

A: Great! I need to _____ tomorrow _____. Can you help?
B: I've been had!

1. generous/borrow a car
2. alert/write a speech
3. calm/cut my hair
4. coordinated/remove the TV antenna from the roof of my house
5. strong/move to a new apartment
6. relaxed/babysit my sister's six children
7. creative/paint my house
8. _____

6 Writing

Are you a lark or an owl? In writing, identify yourself as a lark or an owl and describe your daily routine. Include information about how you feel at different times of the day. Write a first draft, and ask several classmates to read it. Ask them to comment on it and to make suggestions for improvement. Use these comments and suggestions when you write your final draft.

7 Pronunciation

/θ/ /ð/

Repeat these words.

1. think	1. that
2. thanks	2. they
3. bathroom	3. this
4. something	4. brother
5. death	5. other
6. both	6. breathe
	7. bathe

Repeat these contrasting words.

1. teeth   teethe
2. bath   bathe
3. breath   breathe

Now repeat these sentences.

1. They can't go there.
2. They can't go there this Thursday.
3. They can't go there without their mother.
4. I think that's the way to the theater.
5. Theodora thought the third answer was thirty-three thousand.
6. Theodora thought the third answer was thirty-three thousand, but the computer says it's thirty-three thousand and thirteen.

In the Dark

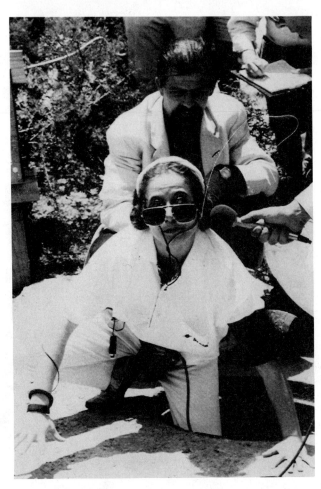

Stefania Follini climbs out of her "room" in the cave after 131 days of isolation.

In 1989, a young Italian designer by the name of Stefania Follini entered a cave near Carlsbad, New Mexico, and stayed there for 131 days. Follini was part of an experiment to determine how isolation and the absence of time cues affect the mind and body. For more than four months, she lived inside the Carlsbad cave in a 20-foot Plexiglas module. While she was living in the cave, she had no way of measuring time. No natural light reached her living space and she had neither a watch nor a clock.

How did Follini react to the isolation? During the first days of the experiment, Follini seemed tense and depressed. She got irritated when researchers outside the cave requested routine reports, and she had trouble concentrating. But this changed as soon as she established a regular routine. As part of this routine, Follini measured her body temperature, heart rate, and blood pressure as soon as she woke up. Researchers above ground received the results through a computer link up. Exercise and breakfast came next in her schedule. Then she filled the rest of the time before lunch by playing cards or playing her guitar and sometimes by drawing. After lunch she read and took a nap. When

she woke up from her nap, she frequently practiced judo (she has a brown belt) and then after supper, she read until she fell asleep.

How were her body rhythms affected during the experiment? When Follini entered the cave, her body rhythms were on a 24-hour cycle. Within a few days, however, this rhythm began to change. She went to bed later and later every night. Eventually she was staying awake for 30 hours at a time and then sleeping for 22 to 24 hours.

The results of this experiment will help researchers learn more about the body's natural rhythms. With this information, researchers may be able to help people adjust to new routines and cope with unusual work schedules and long trips. With a better understanding of body rhythms, we may also find that we have a lot more energy than we realized.

A television camera in the cave shows Follini at her computer.

A Comprehension and Discussion 📼

1. What kind of regular routine did Follini set up while she was in the cave?
2. How did her body react to this living situation?
3. What kinds of problems do you think Follini had while she was living in the cave?
4. What kind of person can best live in isolation for a long period of time?
5. Do you think this was a useful experiment? Why or why not?

Decide if these sentences are true (T) or false (F).

6. This experiment took place in 1989.   T   F
7. The experiment showed that the absence of time cues does not affect the body.   T   F
8. Follini was not able to exercise while she was in the cave.   T   F
9. Her "days" got longer and longer while she was in the cave.   T   F
10. Her body rhythms stayed about the same throughout the experiment.   T   F

B Vocabulary in Context

Fill in the blanks with the correct word. Make any necessary changes in the tense and form of the words. Use each item only once.

Nouns		Verbs	Adjective	Adverb
experiment	isolation	realize	depressed	frequently
absence	routine	cope		
cue		change		

1. Stefania Follini felt _____ when she first entered the cave.
2. The _____ of sunlight can make it difficult to know the time of day.
3. While she was living in the cave, Follini _____ read and played the guitar.
4. Follini's spirits _____ when she began to follow a schedule.
5. Clocks and the sun are types of time _____.
6. As part of her regular _____, she sometimes played cards.
7. The results of this _____ will be useful in planning space travel.
8. _____ affects some people negatively.
9. Follini was able to _____ with life in the cave; she didn't have any big problems during the experiment.
10. Some people don't _____ that body temperature changes during the day.

9 Listening 📼

Listen to the results of a survey on daily schedules and fill in the missing numbers.

I. a. _85%_ of all listeners sleep between 6 and 8 hours a night.

    b. _____ sleep more than 8 hours each night.

    c. _____ sleep fewer than 6 hours a night.

    d. _____ have trouble getting to sleep at night.

II. a. _____ feel drowsy in the afternoon.

    b. _____ take a nap during the day.

III. a. _____ have night or evening jobs.

     b. _____ fell asleep on the job at least once.

10 | Get Together

Play Past Tense Bingo to review past tense verbs. Follow your teacher's instructions.

UNIT 1 VOCABULARY

Nouns		**Verbs**		**Adverbs**
absence	genius	workaholic	reveal	repeat
affect	isolation	**Verbs**	vary	rhythmic
change	nap	adjust	waste	routine
concentration	peak	affect	**Adjectives**	**Adverbs**
coordination	percent	cope	alert	frequently
cue	rhythm	determine	depressed	gradually
cycle	routine	measure	drowsy	sharply
energy	schedule	organize	energetic	**Expressions**
experiment	solution	peak	irritated	I've been had!
findings	success	realize	natural	take a nap
	treatment	request	productive	waste time

Unit One 21

COMMUNICATION
Describing past activities • Asking / answering questions about appointments, schedules • Interviewing • Asking/answering personal questions • Talking about changes over time

GRAMMAR
Present perfect tense • Indefinite time expressions: *ever, never, recently, just* • Indefinite time expressions: *already, yet* • Present perfect continuous tense • Present tense (Review)

Counting Americans

CENSUS '90 **Were You Counted?**

If you believe that you (or anyone else in your household) were NOT counted, please fill out the form below and mail it IMMEDIATELY to:

200 Years of Census Taking

• **I have checked with the members of my household, and I believe that one (or more) of us was NOT counted in the 1990 census.**
• On April 1, 1990, I lived at (PLEASE PRINT)

_____ (Street or road/Rural route and box number)

(House number)

_____ (State)

(Apartment number or location)

_____ (ZIP Code)

(City)

_____ (Street, road, etc.)

(County or foreign country)

• **This address is located between** _____ (Street, road, etc.)

and _____

I am listing **all** persons living in this household on **April 1, 1990**, and those staying or visiting here who had NO other home.

Please list on line **1** the household member who owns, is buying, or rents the home. (PLEASE PRINT)

PLEASE INCLUDE
All family members and othe and babies.
All lodgers, boarders, room
All persons who usually live here but are
trip, on vacation, or in a general hospital.
All persons with a home elsewhere but who stay here most of the week while working or attending college.
Anyone staying or visiting here who had no other home.
All persons in the Armed Forces who l
All children in boarding schools below

DO NOT INCLUDE
Any college student who lives some
Any person away from here in the
a nursing home, mental hospital, o
Any person who usually stays som
Any person visiting here who has

Last name / First name / Middle initial	How is this person related to the person on line 1?	Male or Female	What is the race of this person? (Print name of race grou
	For example: Husband/wife Son/daughter Father/mother Grandchild Mother-in-law Roomer/boarder Housemate/ roommate Unmarried partner Other nonrelative	M or F	White Black or Negro Indian (Amer.) (Also print the na of the enrolled or principal tribe Eskimo Aleut Asian or Pacific Islander (API Chinese Japanese Filipino Asian Ind Hawaiian Samoan Korean Guama Vietnamese Other A Other race (Print race)
1			
2			

A census is the count of a population in a particular area. The United States has had a census every ten years since 1790. Today most people receive a census questionnaire through the mail. Only about five percent of the population— or about 12.5 million people— are interviewed in person.

What questions do you think the 1990 census asked?
Why do countries have a census?

The United States Census

Stand Up and Be Counted

Every ten years the Census Bureau in the United States hires people to count the population. These people are called census takers. For 200 years census takers have climbed mountains, ridden horses, and even flown in helicopters to find and count everyone in the country. Most people have answered their questions politely, but some people have not been so friendly. When a farmer in Texas refused to stop plowing his field, the census taker agreed to ask one question each time the farmer drove by. It took five hours to do the interview. But this kind of persistence pays off. Over the years, the census has been able to keep track of changes in the United States. This information has helped the government and private businesses to make future plans.

What questions does the census ask?

Every census since 1790 has asked the sex and age of each person in the country. Other questions have changed from census to census. Since 1940, however, every census has included questions about housing.

In the 1990 census, five out of six households filled out a short form. This form asked seven questions about each person in the household (such as race, age, and marital status) and seven questions about the housing unit (including whether it is a house or apartment and how many rooms it has). One out of six people filled out a long form with 59 questions. It included questions about education, employment, and income.

How is the information used?

The Congress of the United States is made up of a Senate and a House of Representatives. Each state, whether large or small, has two seats in the Senate. The number of seats in the House of Representatives, however, depends on the state's population. Using information from the census, the government determines how many representatives each state will have. For example, in the 1980s, California, a state with many people, had 45 seats in the House of Representatives. Hawaii, a state with a small population, had two; Alaska, Delaware, North Dakota, South Dakota, Vermont, and Wyoming each had one.

The census data also helps state and local governments to plan community projects such as building new schools and roads. Private businesses study the census figures too. The data helps them to decide on places for new factories or stores. Information about one person or family, however, is always confidential. No one, not even the government, can use information about individuals.

What changes has the census revealed?

The census shows how the United States has changed over the past 200 years. For example, the population of the country has grown from just under 4 million people in 1790 to more than 240 million people today. Since 1820, more than 53 million immigrants have come to the United States. The largest wave of immigrants, nearly 9 million people, came between 1901 and 1910. The census also tells us where these people came from. At the beginning of the century more immigrants came from European countries. Since the 1960s, however, the majority of immigrants have come from countries in South and Central America and from Asia.

The census also gives important information about the economy. For example, census figures show a steady decline in the percent of people working in agriculture. The census of 1820 showed nearly 72 percent of workers doing farm work. By 1950, only 17 percent were on farms. Today, the percent of workers in agriculture has declined to about 3 percent.

A Comprehension and Discussion

1. Why is a census important?
2. How does the U.S. government use the census information?
3. Some people don't like to answer the census questions. Why do you think they feel this way?
4. What kinds of problems do you think a census taker has?
5. People write their names on the census form. Why do you think this is necessary?

B Vocabulary in Context

Choose the word or definition that is closest in meaning to the *italicized* word or phrase.

1. The government uses the census *figures* to plan community projects.
   a. forms   **b.** numbers   **c.** questions
2. Most people *fill out* a short form.
   a. use   **b.** receive   **c.** complete
3. The census helps the government to *keep track of* changes in the economy.
   a. stay informed about   **b.** control   **c.** make use of
4. Private businesses use the census *data* to make business decisions.
   a. facts or numbers   **b.** changes   **c.** economy
5. Agricultural work has *declined* over the past 100 years.
   a. stayed the same   **b.** gone up   **c.** gone down
6. It *pays off* to study a little every day. It does not *pay off* to wait until the day before a test.
   a. costs a lot   **b.** is difficult   **c.** gives good results
7. She was very *persistent;* she worked on the car for 6 hours and finally found the problem.
   a. tired   **b.** determined   **c.** happy
8. Census information is *confidential*.
   a. friendly   **b.** private   **c.** useful

2 Focus on Grammar

Present Perfect Tense
have (has) + past participle

Rule	Example
1. Use the present perfect tense to talk about an event or action that happened at an unspecified time in the past.	a. They **have visited** Italy twice. b. It **has rained** a lot this year.
2. To form the present perfect, use the verb have/has (not)+ a past participle. Regular past participles are formed by adding *-ed* to the simple form of a verb.	a. Many people **have traveled** to the United States from Europe. b. I **haven't looked** at the newspaper today. c. **Have** you **played** that record?
3. Many past participles are not regular, however. You will find a list of common irregular past participles on page 44.	a. They **have been** to Washington three times. b. **Have** you **eaten** in that new restaurant? c. I **have sung** "The Star Spangled Banner" often.
4. The time words *since* and *for* are used with the present perfect tense to show that an activity started in the past and has continued to the present. Use *since* + a specific point in time (since 1980, since 3 a.m.). Use *for* + an amount of time (for two weeks, for several years).	a. He has lived here **since** 1985. (He moved here in 1985 and he is still living here.) b. He has lived here **for** five years. (He moved here five years ago and he is still living here.) BUT They lived in Peru **for** five years. (They don't live in Peru today.)

A Practice

Complete these sentences. Use either the past tense or the present perfect tense.

1. For the past 200 years the census (keep track of) __*has kept track of*__ the changes in the U.S. population.
2. The number of people over 65 in the United States (increase) _____ steadily in the past fifty years.
3. The number of people per household (drop) _____ since 1790.
4. The population of Florida (increase) _____ 43 percent between 1970 and 1980.

5. In 1985, 53 percent of Americans age 65 or older (live) _____ with a spouse.
6. Unemployment (be) _____ at its highest in 1933.
7. Employment in agriculture (decline) _____ since 1950.
8. At the end of 1987, more than 7 million Americans (be) _____ unemployed.
9. Between 1901 and 1985, more than 33 million people (move) _____ to the United States.
10. The Census Bureau (not/be able to) _____ count about 3,171,000 people or 1.4 percent of the population in 1980.

B Practice

Read each sentence below and answer the question that follows with "Yes" or "No." Be prepared to explain your answers.

1. "I lived in the United States for 25 years," answered Greg.
   Does he live in the United States now?
2. Eric asks his friend, "How long have you been in France?"
   Are they in France now?
3. "How long did you live in Chile?" Jean asked.
   Are they in Chile now?
4. "I have worked with Mike for more than five years," explained Jon.
   Do they still work together?
5. "Ben and I worked together five years ago," Jane replied.
   Do Ben and Jane work together now?
6. "I have had a headache all day," complained Bob.
   Does he still have a headache?
7. "I lived on High Street for a year," Danny told Michele.
   Does Danny live on High Street today?
8. "I waited for several hours," he responded.
   Is he still waiting?
9. "How long have you had that car?" Robert asked Sam.
   Does Sam still have the car?
10. "Silvia took care of me for years," Peggy explained.
    Does Silvia still take care of Peggy?

C Interact

You probably don't know how long zippers, pens, and eyeglasses have been around. But can you guess? Work with a partner to try to guess how long we have used the following inventions. Match each statement with its answer. Pay attention to the words *for* and *since*. You can use one answer twice. Then compare your answers with your classmates' answers.

1. Zippers have been around for about _____.
2. The ball-point pen has been in use for _____.
3. People have used toothpaste in tubes since _____.
4. Eyeglasses have been available for _____.
5. People have been taking aspirin since _____.
6. False teeth have been in use for almost _____.
7. The FM radio has been around since _____.
8. Women have worn bikinis since _____.

a. 1946
b. 700 years
c. 1933
d. 1853
e. 2700 years
f. 100 years
g. 1892

(Answers on on page 44)

D Practice

Use the chart to answer the questions about changes in the size of a family in the United States.

Average Number of Persons per Household

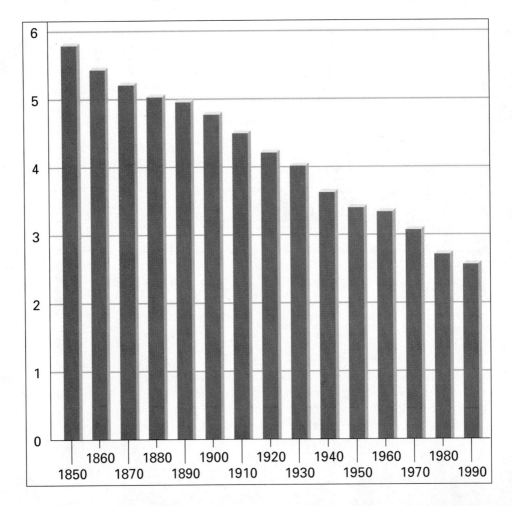

1. How many people were in the average household in 1880?
   In 1880, there were about five people in the average household.
2. Has the number of persons per household increased or decreased since 1880?

3. Did the number of persons per household increase or decrease between 1880 and 1910?

4. In what years was the average number of persons per household below four?

5. Why do you think the number of persons per household has decreased?

E   Interact

The chart below shows the ten largest cities in the United States in 1980. It also shows the population of the cities now. How has the population changed in each city? Has it gone up or down? Use the chart to ask and answer questions about the population in each city.

Examples: What was the population of New York in 1980?

Which city's population has increased the most?

City and State	Population in 1980	Population Now*
New York, NY	7,071,639	7,033,179
Chicago, IL	3,005,072	2,725,979
Los Angeles, CA	2,996,850	3,420,235
Philadelphia, PA	1,688,210	1,543,313
Houston, TX	1,595,138	1,609,723
Detroit, MI	1,203,339	970,156
Dallas, TX	904,078	990,957
San Diego, CA	875,538	1,094,524
Phoenix, AZ	789,704	971,565
Baltimore, MD	786,775	720,100

*Source for "Now": 1990 Postcensus Local Review Tables.

3 Focus on Grammar

Present Perfect Tense with Indefinite Time Expressions
ever, never, just, recently

Rule	Example
1. Use *ever* in a question with the present perfect tense to mean "at any time until now." Use *never* in a statement to mean "not at any time until now."	a. Have you **ever** been to Brazil? b. No, I've **never** been to Brazil.
2. The adverbs *just* and *recently* refer to an indefinite time in the near past. Use the present perfect tense with these adverbs. *Just* usually refers to a nearer time than *recently*.	a. She has **just** returned. b. He has **recently** taken a new job.

A Practice

Complete the sentences with a form of the verb in parentheses. Use the present perfect tense.

1. (never/fill out) I *have never filled out* a census form.
2. (just/pass) The population of the People's Republic of China _____ one billion.
3. (never/travel) I _____ to Asia.
4. (never/take) I _____ the TOEFL, but I will soon.
5. (just/finish) He _____ all of his work.
6. (ever/be) Do you think they _____ to Europe?
7. (see) _____ you _____ him recently?
8. (ever/drive) Do you know if he _____ _____ a car?
9. (ever/try) _____ you _____ the Chinese restaurant down-town?
10. (be) Yes, I _____ there several times recently. The food was great.

B Interact

A: Have you <u>seen any good movies</u> recently?

B: As a matter of fact, I have. I <u>saw *Cinema Paradiso*</u> last week. It was great!

A: Have you _____ recently?

B: As a matter of fact, I have. I _____ last week. It was great!

1. hear/music
2. read/books

3. eat/restaurants
4. read/magazines
5. hear/lectures
6. see/exhibits
7. travel to/places
8. see/TV programs
9. use/computer programs
10. _____

4 | Focus on Grammar

Present Perfect Tense with Indefinite Time Expressions
already, yet

Rule	**Example**
1. The adverb *already* is often used with the present perfect tense in an affirmative statement or in a question. *Already* indicates that something was done before now.	a. I've **already** read that book. b. He's **already** left for school. c. Has he **already** left?
2. The adverb *yet* is often used with the present perfect tense in negative statements or in yes-no questions. Use *yet* to describe something you haven't done but you plan to do soon.	a. I haven't done the dishes **yet**. (But I plan to do them soon.) b. Have you read the newspaper **yet**?

A | Practice

Write your answers to these questions.

1. Have you read that book by Peter Matthiessen yet?
   No I haven't read it yet. (or *Yes, I have already read it.*)
2. Has your teacher given you a test yet?

3. Have you had breakfast yet?

4. Have you seen today's newspaper yet?

5. It's 11 a.m. Have you had lunch already?

6. It's 2 p.m. Have you had lunch yet?

Now write questions for these answers.

7. Yes, they've already bought it.

8. Yes, I've already seen that movie.

9. Yes, he's already done it.

10. Yes, they've already left.

11. Yes, I've already called him.

B **Interact**

Some people keep appointment/schedule books so that they don't forget to do things. This is a page from Marilyn Bloom's appointment book. Look at the time on your watch. Then make questions and answers using *yet* and *already*.

A: Has she <u>had chemistry class</u> yet.
B: Yes, she's already <u>had chemistry class</u>.

A: Has she _____ yet.
B: Yes, she's already _____.

Appointments

8:00 a.m. *Meet Doug for breakfast*
9:00 a.m. *Chemistry class*
10:00 a.m. *Swimming practice*
11:00 a.m.
12:00 a.m. *Lunch*
1:00 p.m. *European History class*
2:00 p.m. *Exam – Math*
3:00 p.m.
4:00 p.m. *Work at Library*
5:00 p.m.
6:00 p.m. *Call home*

5 Focus on Grammar

Present Perfect Continuous Tense
have (has) + been + verb-ing

Rule	Example
1. Both the present perfect tense and the present perfect continuous tense are used to describe an activity that began in the past and has continued to the present. The present perfect continuous tense gives more emphasis to the on-going nature of the activity.	a. They **have been studying** since noon. b. They **have studied** since noon. c. He **hasn't been waiting** for very long. d. He **hasn't waited** for very long.
2. Form the present perfect continuous tense with have/has + been + the present participle. Regular present participles are formed by adding *-ing* to the simple form of a verb.	a. Because of the bad weather, they **have been spending** a lot of time inside. b. She**'s been working** a lot of extra hours.

A | Practice

Use the simple past tense, the past continuous tense, the present perfect, or the present perfect continuous tense in these sentences. Some items have more than one correct answer.

1. I'm going to stop the car soon. I (drive) ___*have driven*___ for more than 4 hours.
2. He (live) _____ in Stockholm when his brother got married.
3. The day after she (arrive) _____ in town, she found a new job.
4. They (have) _____ a lot of trouble with their car lately.
5. Ever since they got a new car, they (take) _____ a lot of trips.
6. She got really angry when she (see) _____ the mess in the kitchen.
7. George Bush (be) _____ the President while my brother was living in the United States.
8. He (sleep) _____ since the movie started.
9. She (buy) _____ tickets as soon as she heard about the concert.
10. For the past two weeks she (read) _____ every book she can find by Annie Dillard.

6 Remember

Present Tense

Rule	Example
Use the present tense to make statements that are generally true.	a. How do most Americans live? b. The average American spends about a third of his or her income on housing.

A Practice

Answer the following questions. Use complete sentences.

1. How old are you?
2. How tall are you?
3. How many credit cards do you have?
4. How many people do you live with?
5. About how many telephone calls do you make a day?
6. Do you have a checking account? If so, how many checks do you write each month?

B Practice

There is no such thing as an "average" person. One can, however, create "statistical pictures" of an average person. The paragraph below uses recent statistics to describe the "average" American woman. Complete the sentences with the correct forms of the verbs in parentheses.

The average American woman (be) _____*is*_____ 5'4" (five feet, four inches or 163cm) tall and (weigh) _____ 144 pounds (65kg). She (have) _____ seven or eight credit

cards and she (drive) _____ to work in an eight-year-old blue sedan. One of her credit cards (be) _____ probably for buying gasoline for her car. She (live) _____ with her husband and two children in a house that is 23 years old. She and her husband (own) _____ the house and together they (spend) _____ two-fifths to one-half of their income on food and shelter. Every month she and her husband (write) _____ 17 checks. On an average day the family members (make) _____ six phone calls.

C Practice

In what ways are you (or a woman friend or relation) similar to the "average" American woman? In what ways are you or she different? Write three sentences about the similarities and differences.

D Practice

Use an appropriate tense of the verb in parentheses to complete these sentences. Some items have more than one correct answer.

1. Roughly 20 percent of all Americans (move) _____*moved*_____ in 1986. The Census Bureau says that the average American (move) _____ at least 11 times in her or his lifetime.
2. In 1987, one out of every five Americans (live) _____ in either New York or California.
3. In the past 50 years, Florida (be) _____ the fastest growing state. By the year 2000, it (be) _____ the third largest state, after California and Texas. The only state that (lose) _____ population since 1970 is New York.
4. 52 percent of Americans now (live) _____ within 50 miles of a coastline. Another 20 percent (live) _____ near the Great Lakes.
5. In 1940, the average American (not/have) _____ a college education. Only one out of four (have) _____ a high school diploma then. In 1985, the average American (have) _____ one year of college. Nearly three out of four (have) _____ a high school diploma. Of those Americans aged 25 – 34, 87 percent (be) _____ high school graduates and 24 percent (have) _____ college degrees.

The following questions appeared on the long form of the 1990 census. Interview another person in your class to get answers to the questions.

At any time since February 1, 1990, has this person attended regular school or college?

O   No, has not attended since February 1

O   Yes, public school, public college

O   Yes, private school, private college

Does this person speak a language other than English at home?

O   Yes

O   No
If yes, what is the language?

_____

(For example: Chinese, Italian, Spanish, Vietnamese)

How well does this person speak English?

O   Very well   O   Not well

O   Well   O   Not at all

Has this person been on active-duty military service in the Armed Forces of the United States or ever been in the United States military Reserves or the National Guard?

O   Yes, now on active duty

O   Yes, on active duty in past, but not now

O   Yes, service in Reserves or National Guard only

O   No

CENSUS '90

7 Pronunciation

/k/ /g/

Repeat these words.

1. cake
2. chemistry
3. king
4. account
5. architect
6. acknowledge
7. check
8. music
9. take

Now repeat these words.

1. game
2. guide
3. ghost
4. beggar
5. begin
6. magazine
7. rug
8. bug
9. vogue

Repeat these contrasting words.

1. good	could
2. dug	duck
3. game	came
4. gold	cold

Repeat these sentences.

1. I'd like to ask you a couple of questions.
2. I'd like to ask you a couple of questions concerning folk music.
3. To become a chemist you have to get a college degree.
4. To become a chemist, you have to get a college degree and take many courses in chemistry.

Case Study #1:

The City of Strafford

The city of Strafford receives money from the state government based on the city's total population. Since the last census count, the city has received $140 per person per year.

In the past few years, the economy of the area has not been good. A few companies have gone out of business, and a few hundred people have lost their jobs. Most of these people, however, have stayed in Strafford. At the time of the census, the city government believed that the population was still about 100,000 residents. When the new census counted the people, however, it came up with only 98,500 residents. Because of this decline in population, Strafford will lose about $210,000 per year, or more than $2 million for the decade. To make ends meet, the city will need to cut its budget. The fire and police departments, the local hospital, transportation services, and public welfare programs will all get less money.

A **Comprehension and Discussion**

1. What changes have taken place in Strafford since the last census?
2. Has the population gone up or down?
3. Why is Strafford going to receive less money from the government?
4. What will the city do to make ends meet?
5. Why do you think there was a decline in the city's population? What do you think the city can do to prevent another decline in the next census?

Case Study #2:

The Town of Fay Creek

The town of Fay Creek has received money from the state for four new projects: a public swimming pool, a small park, a new senior citizens recreation center, and one new bus route. A private health care company also wants to open a new medical center in Fay Creek.

The town will use data from the census report to help find the best places to locate these facilities and the best route for the bus line. The census report cuts an area into tracts, or pieces of land. It then gives information for each tract. Chart A below shows the town of Fay Creek divided into sixteen census tracts. Each tract has a number. Chart B shows how many children live in each tract. It also shows how many people age 65 or older and how many people without cars live in each tract.

Chart A

1	*2*	*3*	*4*
5	*6*	*7*	*8*
9	*10*	*11*	*12*
13	*14*	*15*	*16*

Chart B

Census Tract	Number of Children	Number of People 65+	Adults Without Cars
1	816	89	35
2	743	122	88
3	51	98	65
4	123	65	235
5	645	142	107
6	156	154	89
7	65	74	214
8	45	63	142
9	56	503	282
10	224	414	243
11	178	366	199
12	215	42	46
13	67	123	87
14	132	16	67
15	342	24	39
16	214	11	55

B Comprehension and Discussion

1. Use the information in the charts to make the following decisions: In which census tract do you want to locate (a) the swimming pool, (b) the park, (c) the senior citizens recreation center, and (d) the medical center? Think about who will use each of these facilities and where they live. Locate each facility on Chart A.
2. How did you decide on the location for the small park?
3. Now decide on the best route for the new bus line. It will go from one side of town to the other. Draw a line on Chart A to show the bus line.

C Vocabulary in Context

Fill in the blanks with the correct word. Make any necessary changes in the form and tense of the verbs.

Nouns	Verbs
data	make ends meet
recreation	cut
economy	stay
decades	
budget	

1. Sometimes it's not easy _____; I usually don't have any money left at the end of the month.
2. It's useful to make a _____. It tells you what you can afford to buy.
3. For _____, I often go swimming or sailing.
4. My boss _____ my pay because I was late so many times.
5. A century, or one hundred years, is made up of ten _____.
6. Computers can hold a lot more _____ than the human brain can.
7. The cost of living _____ about the same since last year.
8. When the _____ is bad in an area, unemployment rises.

9 New Expressions: Phrasal Verbs

Fill in the blanks with a phrasal verb. Use each verb in the correct form. You may use a verb more than once.

Separable	
fill out	*complete a form or application*

Inseparable	
keep track (of)	*keep informed about someone or something*
pay off	*be successful*
come up (with)	*think of an answer; produce*

1. It doesn't usually _____ to stay up all night to study for a test.
2. If you are tired, you may not be able to _____ with the right answers on the test.
3. If you want to apply to the university, you must _____ these forms.
4. If you want to _____ of appointments, you should write them down.
5. You should probably _____ this form _____ before you leave.

10 Writing

Imagine that you are opening a restaurant. You can open this restaurant anywhere in your town. First, decide what kind of restaurant it will be. For example, will it serve cheap or expensive meals? What kind of food will it serve? Will it serve dinner only? Write a short description of your restaurant. Then, make up a questionnaire to help you find the best area for your restaurant. What information would help you to choose a location?

When, you have written a first draft of your description and questionnaire, let several of your classmates read it and comment on it. Use their comments and suggestions to write a final draft of the description and questionnaire. Proofread carefully, paying special attention to punctuation and spelling.

11 Listening 📼

Many businesses and government agencies collect information. You are going to hear some typical questions. Listen to the question and then circle the best answer a person could give to it. Only one of the choices answers the question.

1. **a.** three
   b. Yes, I do.
   c. Yes, I like children very much.

2. **a.** three people
   b. many times
   c. three years

3. **a.** one year
   b. No, thank you.
   c. Yes, I do.

4. **a.** about two
   b. I have two TVs.
   c. usually in the morning

5. **a.** in New York
   b. last year
   c. three years ago

6. **a.** It's my second marriage.
   b. next year
   c. for three years

7. **a.** less than
   b. $24,000
   c. Yes, I do.

8. **a.** for four years
   b. Yes, I am.
   c. Yes, I do.

12 | Get Together

Work with your classmates to make a list of changes that have taken place in the city or town where you live now. Interview several people who have lived in the city or town for a long time to find out what changes they have seen. Report your findings to the rest of the class.

UNIT 2 VOCABULARY

Nouns			
budget	data	facility	income
census	decade	figure	individual
century	economy	household	lifetime
	employment	immigrant	majority

marital status
persistence
population
questionnaire
recreation
resident
unemployment
welfare

Verbs
count

cut
decline
hire
include
locate
stay
vary

Adjectives
average
confidential

local
persistent
total

Adverbs
already
just
nearly
politely
recently
yet

Phrasal Verbs
fill out
keep track (of)
pay off
come up (with)

Expressions
depend on
go out of business
make ends meet

IRREGULAR VERBS: PAST PARTICIPLES

Base Form	Past Participle	Base Form	Past Participle
be	been	lie	lied
become	become	lose	lost
begin	begun	make	made
blow	blown	mean	meant
break	broken	meet	met
bring	brought	mistake	mistaken
build	built	overcome	overcome
buy	bought	pay	paid
catch	caught	put	put
choose	chosen	quit	quit
come	come	read	read (pronounced "red")
cost	cost	ride	ridden
do	done	ring	rung
drink	drunk	rise	risen
drive	driven	run	run
eat	eaten	say	said
fall	fallen	see	seen
feed	fed	sell	sold
feel	felt	send	sent
fight	fought	show	shown
find	found	shrink	shrunk
fly	flown	shut	shut
forget	forgotten	sing	sung
freeze	frozen	sit	sat
get	gotten (or got)	sleep	slept
give	given	speak	spoken
go	gone	spend	spent
grow	grown	stand	stood
have	had	steal	stolen
hear	heard	swim	swum
hide	hidden	take	taken
hit	hit	teach	taught
hold	held	tell	told
hurt	hurt	think	thought
kccp	kept	throw	thrown
leave	left	understand	understood
lend	lent	wear	worn
let	let	win	won
lie (recline)	lain	write	written

Answers to exercise C, pages 27-28: 1f, 2f, 3g, 4b, 5d, 6e, 7c, 8a

UNIT 3

COMMUNICATION
Discussing fashions and fads • Asking/
answering questions about attitudes, abilities • Interviewing • Asking/answering
probing questions • Explaining choices,
preferences • Expressing surprise

GRAMMAR
Gerunds • Infinitives • Verbs followed
by infinitives and gerunds • Present
perfect tense (Review)

Fads

The dictionary defines a fad as a fashion, custom, or amusement that keeps people's attention for a short time.

Each of the pictures on this page shows something that was a fad in the United States in this century. Can you identify the fads? Were any of these a fad in your country?

Why do you think people do these crazy things?

Did People Really Do These Crazy Things?

Flagpoles and Phone Booths

He called himself the "Luckiest Fool Alive." His name was Alvin Kelley and one day in 1924, he climbed to the top of a theater flagpole in Hollywood, California. He ended up staying there for 13 hours and 13 minutes and getting a lot of attention. Soon after, other people were trying to break his pole sitting record.

Who knows how or why fads get started? Roger Price didn't plan to start a fad in 1953. He simply wanted Garry Moore, the popular TV emcee, to show the audience a group of his unusual drawings,

Alvin Kelley on top of a flagpole in New York City

or "droodles." When Moore showed the droodles on TV, the audience went crazy trying to guess what the drawings were. Over the next week, Price received more than 15,000 fan letters. People started making their own droodles, and high school kids began making their own versions, called "Living Droodles."

Some fads have a good marketing person behind them, someone who can sell even the dumbest idea to the public. Gary Dahl is one of these people, and he is now a very wealthy man. In 1975, Dahl heard some of his friends complaining about problems with their pets. Dahl started joking about his perfect pet. His pet did not cause any trouble and it never made a mess. It was a rock. Dahl's friends were amused by his joke and this convinced him to act on the idea. By Christmas of that year, pet rocks were on the market and selling like crazy.

Some fads are pretty ridiculous. In the 1930s, people who enjoyed dancing got involved in crazy contests called dance marathons. People danced for days and weeks without stopping. Whoever could dance the longest won the contest. In the 1950s, American kids

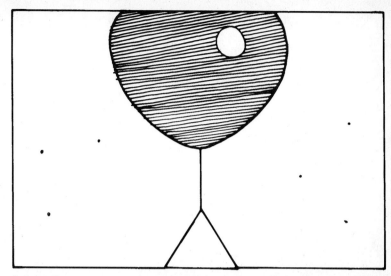

A droodle

got excited about stuffing themselves into phone booths. Groups of students tried to outdo each other by getting more people into such a tiny space.

It may be true that fads abound when times are hard—when the economy is in trouble. The 1958 recession caused the Hula

Hoop mania, some people say. Maybe it's true, or maybe people just like to do something crazy once in a while.

A Comprehension and Discussion

1. What are the characteristics of a fad?
2. Why do you think Alvin Kelley chose to stay at the top of a flagpole for such a long time?
3. Why do you think people bought pet rocks?
4. Are fads ever dangerous?
5. Do you think it is possible to convince people to buy anything?
6. Do you agree that fads appear when times are difficult? Why or why not?

B Vocabulary

Match each word on the left with an appropriate definition on the right.

1. _____ version   a. management of a country's resources
2. _____ ridiculous   b. entertain; make laugh
3. _____ complain   c. disorder; dirty or untidy condition
4. _____ mess   d. different form of something
5. _____ amuse   e. silly
6. _____ economy   f. temporary decline in economic activity
7. _____ recession   g. stupid
8. _____ marathon   h. express dissatisfaction
9. _____ dumb   i. do better than
10. _____ outdo   j. contest of endurance

2 Focus on Grammar

Using gerunds
verb -ing

Rule	Example
1. A gerund is a noun made out of a verb. It is the simple form of the verb + *-ing*.	swimming, singing, studying
2. A gerund can be the subject of a sentence.	a. **Bicycling** was a popular fad in the late 1800s. b. **Rollerskating** became popular in the 1890s. <div align="right">(continued)</div>

Using Gerunds (continued)

Rule	Example
3. A gerund can be the object of certain verbs: *appreciate, avoid, delay, deny, discuss, dislike, enjoy, finish, mind, miss, practice, quit, have trouble, regret, spend time, stop, try.*	a. In the 1920s, many people **enjoyed watching** dance marathons b. By the 1960s kids had **stopped playing** with Hula Hoops. c. I wouldn't **mind seeing** that movie.
4. A gerund can be the object of a preposition. Common expressions with prepositions are: *be afraid of, become accustomed to, be careful about, get excited about, get used to, be interested in, look forward to, be nervous about, talk about, get tired of, be good at, think about.*	a. In the early 1930s, many people got excited **about playing** a new game called Monopoly. b. When people got tired **of playing** with Hula-Hoops, the fad died out. c. She's really interested **in learning** how to fly a plane.

A **Practice**

Complete these sentences by adding a gerund or a phrase with a gerund.

1. She is afraid of _____*making a mistake*_____.
2. When I take a trip, I look forward to _____.
3. _____ is popular today.
4. I am not at all interested in _____.
5. In the morning, I really enjoy _____.
6. Last weekend I spent a lot of time _____.
7. I think people should be more careful about _____.
8. Children look forward to _____.
9. When I was a child, I disliked _____.
10. I don't think I'm very good at _____.
11. I will never get tired of _____.
12. I don't think I will ever get used to _____.
13. I am really looking forward to _____.
14. On a rainy day I really don't mind _____.
15. For our vacation, we have been thinking about _____.
16. So far, I have been able to avoid _____.
17. She's trying very hard to stop _____.
18. Have you ever thought about _____.

Practice these dialogues with a partner. Add a preposition and a gerund to complete each of the sentences.

1. (wear)
   A: I'm really tired __of wearing__ short skirts. I can't wait for long skirts to become popular again.
   B: I don't agree. It seems as if you just get used _____ short skirts and the fad dies out.

2. (do)
   A: I don't think I'll ever be good _____ crossword puzzles. I think I'll give up trying.
   B: Oh, come on. You look forward _____ the crossword puzzle in the newspaper every day. Today's puzzle is just an unusually difficult one.

3. (fly)
   A: Tell me the truth. Are you nervous _____ in airplanes?
   B: To tell the truth, I've really gotten used _____. But I was nervous at first.

4. (get)
   A: I really don't understand why people got excited _____ into a phone booth with a lot of other people. That was a crazy fad.
   B: Yeah, I would be afraid _____ into a phone booth with thirty-four other people. You wouldn't be able to move.

5. (use)
   A: How long does it take to become accustomed _____ a computer? I've been working on this computer for a week and I still haven't gotten used to it.
   B: Don't worry, you'll get used _____ it pretty soon. It just takes time.

3 Focus on Grammar

Using Infinitives
to + the simple form of the verb

Rule	Example
1. An infinitive is formed with *to* + the simple form of the verb.	to swim, to sing, to study
2. Infinitives can follow these verbs: *afford, agree, ask, decide, demand, expect, forget, hope, learn, need, plan, promise, refuse, seem, wait, want, wish.*	a. Some people **hope to make** money from fads. b. He **refuses to do** what everyone else is. c. Kids **want to be** like their friends; they **want to do** what their friends are doing.
3. These verbs are followed by a noun or pronoun and then an infinitive: *advise, allow, convince, encourage, force, invite, order, permit, teach, tell, warn.*	a. Few people **expected** pet rocks **to become** a fad. b. In the 1960s, advertisements **encouraged** women **to wear** miniskirts. c. In the 1950s, schools did not **permit** girls **to wear** pants.
4. These verbs can be followed by a noun or pronoun and an infinitive or by an infinitive alone: *ask, expect, need, want.*	a. He **asked to go** to the dance. b. He **asked** me **to go** to the dance. c. I **expect to go** to the dance. d. I **expect** her **to go** to the dance.

A Interact

Get some information about one of your classmates. Write your classmate's answers on your paper.

1. What do you plan to do tonight?
   I plan to go out with my friends.
2. What do you need to do this weekend?

3. Can you afford to live without working?

4. What would you warn young children to watch out for?

5. What do you expect the government to do for you?

6. What place in your country would you advise a tourist to visit?

7. Is there anyone you would refuse to help?

8. Are there any languages you want to learn to speak?

9. What do you expect to learn in this class?

10. How could you convince someone to buy a pet rock?

B **Practice**

Complete these sentences with the verbs in parentheses. Use either a gerund or an infinitive.

1. (sit)
   A: Would you agree _____*to sit*_____ on a flag pole?
   B: No way. I'm not in the least bit interested in _____
      on a flagpole. That's a crazy idea.
2. (buy)
   A: No sensible person would consider _____ a pet rock?
   B: I agree, but Gary Dahl was able to convince a lot of people
      _____ one in 1975.
3. (lend)
   A: Do you think you could convince your brother _____ you his
      car?
   B: Lend me his car? You must be crazy. My brother wouldn't consider
      _____ me his car.
4. (eat)
   A: You know, I don't think we can afford _____ in this restaurant.
   B: Well, I don't mind _____ somewhere else. Let's look for a
      cheaper place.
5. (watch)
   A: I'm really tired of _____ these dumb advertisements on TV.
   B: If you don't want _____ them, why don't you just get up, go to
      the kitchen, and get me something to drink?

4 Focus on Grammar

Verbs followed by infinitives or gerunds

Rule	Example
Infinitives or gerunds can follow these verbs: *begin, can't stand, continue, hate, like, love, prefer, start, try.*	a. Government officials **tried prohibiting** dance marathons in the 1930s. b. Government officials **tried to prohibit** dance marathons.

A Interact

Complete these four lists. Then follow the instructions below.

*Two things I like
to do alone*

*Two things I like
to do with my hands*

*Two things I like to do
that don't cost anything*

*Two things I like to do
on a rainy day*

Spend two minutes talking to your partner about one of the items on your list. Explain why you like to do the activity.

B Get Together

Write five sentences about yourself. One of the sentences must be untrue. Use gerunds or infinitives in your sentences.

Example:
I love to read.
I enjoy studying English.
I want to learn to speak Chinese.
I like to swim.
I hate dancing.

Show your list to each of your classmates. Write down the names of your classmates who guessed which of your sentences was a lie.

C Interact

Phrases like *Is that right? Really?* and *No kidding?* help to keep conversations going because they encourage people to give you more information. Practice this dialogue with a partner.

A: I <u>hate watching TV</u>.
B: Really?

A: Yeah. It's <u>boring. You just sit there and get fat</u>. What about you?
B: To be honest, <u>I enjoy watching TV but I also like to do things outside</u>.

A: I _____.
B: _____?

A: Yeah. It's _____. What about you?
B: To be honest, I _____.

5 Writing

Droodles were a fad in the 1950s. Work with several of your classmates to write an explanation of these drawings and photograph. Then draw one of your own droodles and share it with your classmates.

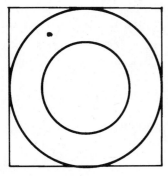 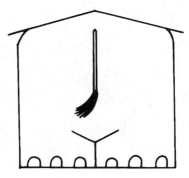 

6 Pronunciation

/f/ /v/

Repeat these words.

1. found
2. few
3. flowers
4. safari
5. difficult

6. telephone
7. photograph
8. safe
9. stiff
10. enough

Now repeat these words.

1. view	**6.** divide
2. very	**7.** five
3. variety	**8.** have
4. every	**9.** I've
5. adventure	

Repeat these contrasting words.

1. fine	vine
2. fan	van
3. few	view
4. fat	vat

Now repeat these sentences.

1. Fifteen people went on the safari adventure.
2. They found a great variety of vegetation.
3. A few people took photographs.
4. A few people took photographs of the flowers and the vines.
5. Many Vermont farms have fine views.

A Vermont farm

Keep On Dancing

Marathon dancers learned to sleep while dancing.

After forty-five minutes of dancing the bell rang. The dancers left the dance floor and slowly headed for the beds in the next room. Fifteen minutes later, the bell rang again and the weary dancers struggled back to the dance floor. All day and all night, the same dancers continued to dance. Weeks passed and they kept on dancing. They were called dance marathons and people were crazy about them in the 1930s. In the longest marathon, the dancing went on for 5,148 hours or nearly 215 days.

It was just after the stock market crash of 1929 in the United States. The Great Depression that followed affected everyone, and thousands of people were out of jobs. For some young people, entering a dance marathon was simply a way to earn money for food. As long as they continued to dance, they got food to eat.

The first 500 hours of a dance marathon were the most difficult. Dancers had to get used to sleeping while leaning on their partners. Feet got sore and swollen, and tempers flared as dancers got tired. Three times a day, tables were pulled out onto the dance floor and the dancers ate — while dancing.

For many people, watching a dance marathon was a cheap form of entertainment. At any time of day or night they could go and watch the dancers in the marathon. They yelled and threw money at their favorite dancers to encourage them to keep dancing. Some made bets on who would quit or fall down next.

Dancers in a marathon were pushed to their limits. Without proper sleep, many got sick. When several dancers died from overexertion in a 1929 dance marathon, government officials tried unsuccessfully to outlaw marathons. Instead, marathons continued to be popular until the United States entered World War II. The wartime economy brought the country out of the Depression and people finally began to lose interest in dance marathons.

Dancers ate while they danced.

A | Comprehension and Discussion

1. Would you participate in a dance marathon? Why or why not?
2. What was the economic situation of the United States when dance marathons became popular?
3. In what way were dance marathons dangerous?
4. Why do you think they were so popular?
5. How did the dancers in a marathon rest?
6. How did the dancers make money?
7. Why did officials try to outlaw dance marathons?
8. When did people stop going to dance marathons?

B | Vocabulary in Context

Fill in the blanks with the correct word or expression. Make any necessary changes in the form and tense of the verbs. Use each item only once.

Nouns	Verbs	Adjectives
limit	lean	weary
partner	yell	sore
	overexert	cheap
	earn	
	struggle	

1. After dancing for two months, she was extremely _____.
2. Dancers in a marathon _____ enough money to pay for their food.
3. Dancers _____ on their partners when they wanted to sleep.
4. If you walk or dance for a long time, your feet get _____.
5. It didn't cost much to watch a dance marathon. The tickets were _____.
6. She reached her _____ after 300 hours of dancing. She couldn't dance anymore after that.
7. Be careful not to _____ yourself in this hot weather. Working too hard in this heat can make you sick.
8. In a dance marathon, a dancer kept the same _____ for the entire contest.
9. There's a lot of noise. He might hear you if you _____.
10. It's not easy to stay awake all night. You really have to _____ to keep your eyes open.

8 Remember

Have you ever been in a dance marathon?
They have just started dancing.

A Practice

Read this letter from a dancer in a marathon. Underline the verbs in the present perfect tense.

> Dear Dotti,
>   Well, I only have fifteen minutes to write because when the bell rings, I have to start dancing again. We've danced for just over 1,000 hours now and believe me, my feet are sore and I'm very tired. I haven't had a good night's sleep in more than a month. Between dances, you only have 15 minutes to sleep. As soon as you fall asleep, the bell rings again. Of course I've been able to sleep on the dance floor. I can sleep as long as my partner stays awake and keeps me from falling down!
>   I know you think I'm crazy for doing this, but really it's kind of interesting. People come and watch us every day, and I've even earned a good amount of money. And if I win the contest, I will get one thousand dollars. That's more money than I have ever seen. Tell mom that I'm eating well and that I'll be home soon.
>
>   June

9 Listening 📼

Listen to the conversations. Then answer these questions.

Conversation #1
a. What is the woman trying to discourage the man from doing?
b. Why does he want to do this activity?

Conversation #2
a. What did the man like about the dance marathon?
b. What did he dislike about it?

Conversation #3
a. Who convinced the boy to get his hair cut?
b. Why did he cut his hair?

Conversation #4
a. What does the woman want her son to do?
b. What does he want to do?

Coversation #5
a. What does the man want to buy?
b. Who is he going to give it to?

10 Get Together

What are some popular fads today? Do you think young people get more involved in fads than older people do? If so, why?

Talk to some people who are older than you. Find out what fads existed when they were growing up. Report your findings to the rest of the class.

UNIT 3 VOCABULARY

Nouns	recession	deny	ridiculous
attention	record	earn	sore
audience	space	lean	swollen
contest	trouble	outdo	wealthy
economy	version	overexert	weary
entertainment		regret	
fad	_Verbs_	struggle	_Expressions_
limit	abound	stuff	end up
mania	act	yell	go crazy
marathon	affect		sell like crazy
market	amuse	_Adjectives_	be interested in
mess	appreciate	cheap	get tired of
outlaw	avoid	dumb	look forward to
overexertion	break	perfect	can't stand
partner	complain	popular	head for
pet	convince		

UNIT 4

COMMUNICATION
Using analogies • Discussing pros and cons of possible future actions • Suggesting alternative explanations and solutions • Discussing problem solving

GRAMMAR
Future possible conditional statements • Modals to express possibility: *may, might, could, can* • Verb tenses (Review)

Creativity

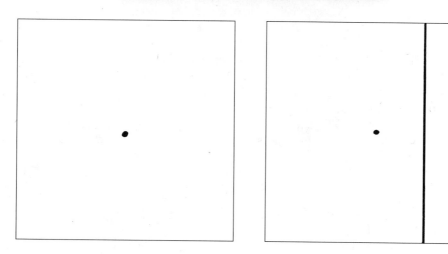

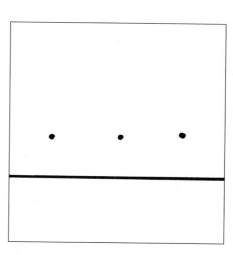

Think of someone who is very creative. What makes you think he or she is a creative person? How would you describe creative people in general?

What do you see in each of these pictures? What could it show or represent?

What does the word *cold* make you think of? Perhaps it makes you think of ice, a refrigerator, the Arctic, or anything else that's cold. What do these words make you think of? Write as many things as you can that each one brings to your mind or makes you think of: *tall, soft, aunt*.

Creativity Tips

"I'm not a very creative person."
"Creativity is only for artists and inventors."
"I haven't had an original idea in years."

If you have doubts about your creative abilities, you might want to listen to the experts on creative thinking. According to these researchers, people can learn to be more creative. Here are some of their suggestions:

TRY BRAINSTORMING. This technique might help you to come up with creative ideas. In brainstorming, you write down every idea that comes into your head— even if it seems crazy or silly. But don't judge the ideas. Judging each idea might make you

Tabatha Babbett invented the circular saw by putting together the ideas of two common items, the spinning wheel and the straight saw.

freeze up. Instead, relax and allow your mind to be playful. After you have come up with a long list of ideas, you can then go back and choose the best one.

GET IDEAS FROM THE THINGS AROUND YOU. If you are looking for a new idea, you might try combining things that already exist. Tabatha Babbett used this method to come up with the idea for a circular saw. One day, she was working at her spinning wheel and watching two men at work outside. The men were having trouble cutting wood with a straight saw. Babbett made the connection between her spinning wheel and the job of cutting wood. Using a circular saw might make it easier to cut the wood, she thought.

MAKE ANALOGIES. If you are looking for a new way to solve a problem, you could try making analogies. In the 1870s, the inventor Eli Whitney was looking for an easy way to pull the seeds out of cotton. One day he saw a cat trying to catch a chicken through a fence. The cat put its paw through the fence and waited for the chicken to walk by. The cat didn't catch the chicken, but it did get a pawful of feathers. Something clicked in Whitney's mind and he saw the similarity between the cat's action and the problem he was trying to solve. A machine called the cotton gin resulted from this analogy.

BREAK THE RULES. Sticking to rules that no longer make sense might prevent you from coming up with new ideas. Nolan Bushnell, the inventor of the first video game, was trying to find new ideas for pinball games. In the existing games, the playing field was always 26 inches wide. As long as Bushnell followed this rule, he had trouble being creative. However, when he finally gave up that rule and made the field 30 inches wide, he was able to come up with many new ideas.

DON'T GIVE UP. When Thomas Edison was trying to make the first light bulb, he used seven thousand different materials before he finally found the right one. Perhaps this is why he said that genius was "ninety-nine percent perspiration and one percent inspiration."

A cat and a chicken helped Eli Whitney come up with the idea for the "cotton gin," a machine to remove the seeds from cotton.

A Comprehension and Discussion

1. What is the main purpose of this article?
2. In the paragraph about brainstorming, what do you think the term *freeze up* means?
3. According to the article, how did Tabatha Babbett get the idea for the circular saw?
4. What is an anology? Can you give an example of an anology?
5. What did Edison mean in his definition of genius?
6. Do you know any other techniques for creative problem solving?
7. If you are having trouble coming up with an idea, what do you usually do?

B Vocabulary in Context

Choose the correct answer to complete the sentence.

1. Jacob thinks that his brother is an *expert* on rock and roll music. He says, _____.
   a. "My brother likes rock and roll music."
   b. "My brother knows a lot about this kind of music."
   c. "My brother hates this music."
2. If the instructions tell you to *combine* flour and water, you should _____.
   a. put the flour and water in separate bowls
   b. cook the flour and water
   c. put them together
3. My answer didn't *make sense* to Carlos. He said, _____.
   a. "I don't understand your answer. Could you explain it to me?"
   b. "I agree with you completely."
   c. "I didn't think you knew that."
4. Sarah is having trouble *sticking* to her work. She says, _____.
   a. "I can't stop working."
   b. "I can't continue working."
   c. "It's hard to understand my work."
5. Piero is having trouble *coming up* with an idea for his paper. He says, _____.
   a. "I can't decide which idea to choose."
   b. "I don't like any of my ideas."
   c. "I can't think of any ideas."
6. After looking for his wallet for several hours, Jeff finally *gave up*. He said, _____.
   a. "I'll never find my wallet."
   b. "I'll give you my wallet."
   c. "I'm glad I found my wallet."

Vocabulary

Complete these sentences with the correct form of the word. Make any necessary changes in the form of the verbs.

1. *judgment judge*
   a. Before you make a _____, you might want to hear his side of the story.
   b. He couldn't _____ how far away the car was.
2. *combinations combine*
   a. The cake tasted funny because she didn't _____ the ingredients well.
   b. Words are made of different _____ of letters.
3. *connection connect*
   a. Two parallel lines will never _____.
   b. There is no _____ between these ideas.
4. *action act*
   a. For every _____, there is a reaction.
   b. If you don't _____ quickly, someone else might take the job.
5. *invention invent*
   a. Everyone was excited about his new _____.
   b. His sister _____ a new kind of toy.

2 Focus on Grammar

Future Possible Conditional Statements
If + present tense (future meaning)

Rule	Example
	"if" clause *result clause*
1. A future possible conditional statement is made up of an *if* clause and a *result* clause. Use a future possible conditional statement to describe what will happen in the future if certain conditions exist.	a. **If you relax**, you will probably come up with a solution to your problem. b. **If I have time tomorrow**, I'll finish that book.
2. To form the future possible conditional, use the present tense in the *if* clause. You can then use *will* or *won't* + the simple form of the verb in the *result* clause.	a. If you **need** a ride tomorrow, I **will pick** you up. b. If you **don't like** it, I **won't buy** any more.
	(continued)

Future Possible Conditional Statements (continued)

3. Modal auxiliaries are often used in the result clause instead of *will* or *won't*.	**a.** If you want to improve something, you **might** try combining things in a new way. **b.** If you need something, you **can** call.

4. The imperative mood is sometimes used in the result clause.	**a.** If it is possible, **put** yourself in a playful mood. **b.** If you go to the store, **get** some milk.

5. The *if* clause can go at the beginning or at the end of the sentence.	**a.** **If your idea fails**, try something else. **b.** Try something else **if your idea fails**.

A Practice

Complete each sentence, using the verb in parentheses. Be sure to change the form of the verb if necessary.

(think) **1.** If you _____*think*_____ of something unrelated to the problem, you might find a solution.

(be) **2.** It will be easier to get new ideas if you _____ relaxed.

(leave) **3.** If he _____ by 9 tonight, he will get there on time.

(need) **4.** If you _____ some money next week, let me know.

(fail) **5.** If you _____ the first time, don't give up.

(help) **6.** If you help me with this tomorrow, I _____ you next week.

(call) **7.** Just _____ me if you get lost on your way to my house.

(find) **8.** You _____ a solution to the problem if you keep trying. Don't give up!

(leave) **9.** If you keep on arguing with your brother, I _____.

(eat) **10.** If he doesn't get here in the next few minutes, we _____ without him.

B Practice

Complete these sentences with appropriate clauses.

1. If we don't find a cure for AIDS, ___*many more people will die*___.

2. If the world population continues to increase, _____.

3. If we continue to pollute the oceans, _____.

4. If you don't learn to relax, _____.

5. If you want to stay warm, _____.

6. If you want to cool off, _____.

7. If you are having trouble being creative, _____.

8. If you don't like the music on the radio, _____.

9. If you can't remember someone's phone number, _____.

10. If you need a quiet place to study, _____.

C | Practice

American parents sometimes threaten their kids with statements like this: *If you spend all your money, I won't give you any more,* **or** *If you don't get your hair out of your eyes, I'll cut it off.* **What do you think the parents might say in the situations below? Complete the sentences with appropriate clauses.**

1. If you hit your brother again, _*I won't let you go to the party*_ .

2. If you don't do your homework, _____.

3. If you don't sit up straight, _____.

4. If you two don't stop fighting, _____.

5. If you don't turn off the TV and go to bed right now, _____.

6. If you don't clean up your room, _____.

7. If I catch you smoking, _____.

8. If your grades don't improve, _____.

9. If you're not home in time for dinner, _____.

10. If you say that word again, _____.

Practice this dialogue with a partner.

A: Did I tell you? I'm thinking of <u>sailing across the ocean</u>.

B: <u>Sailing across the ocean</u>! That's crazy. What if <u>you get lost</u>?

A: That's not a problem. If I <u>get lost</u>, I'll <u>use my radio to get information</u>.

A: Did I tell you? I'm thinking of _____.

B: _____! That's crazy. What if _____?

A: That's not a problem. If I _____, I'll _____.

1. driving across the country
2. taking a new job
3. going to Caracas to study Spanish
4. learning to fly an airplane
5. taking a job in Brazil
6. swimming across the English Channel
7. starting a newspaper
8. cutting my hair really short
9. writing a story about you
10. _____

3 Grammar in Focus

Models to Express Possibility
may, might, could, can

Rule	Example
Use the modals *may, might,* or *could* to suggest possibilities. *May* expresses a little more certainty than *might. Can* is sometimes used informally to suggest possibility.	a. You **might** freeze up if you start judging your ideas right away. b. Relaxing **may** help you to think better. c. I **may** go to the movies tonight. d. Thinking of something unrelated to the problem **could** help you to get an idea. e. He **could** be at his brother's house. f. Relaxing **can** help you to come up with new ideas.

A | Practice

Can you give a possible explanation or a suggestion for these problems? Write your ideas on your paper. Use *may, might, could,* or *can* in your answers.

> *Example:* I just can't come up with an original idea. What's wrong with me today?
> *You might not be relaxed.*

1. I haven't gotten a phone call in three days. What could be the matter?

2. The trees around my house are dying. What might be the problem?

3. There is a policeman following me. I can't imagine what I'm doing wrong.

4. My car won't start. What could be wrong?

5. My neighbors are driving me crazy. They have loud parties almost every night. Is there any way to get them to be quieter?

6. A friend of mine needs money, but I know he's too proud to ask me for a loan. Is there any way I can help him?

7. I've decided to start a language school but I can't think of a name for it. Do you have any ideas?

8. I own a store that sells records and tapes. I'm looking for ideas to get more customers into my store. Do you have any suggestions?

B | Interact

Practice this dialogue with a partner.

A: Mark <u>didn't show up for work</u> today. I wonder what's wrong.
B: That's strange. I suppose he may (might) <u>be sick</u>.
A: That's possible. He may (might) <u>also be out having fun</u>.

A: Mark _____ today. I wonder what's wrong.
B: That's strange. I suppose he may (might) _____.
A: That's possible. He may (might) _____.

1. left early
2. looked very unhappy
3. wouldn't talk to me
4. got here late
5. has refused to eat anything
6. is taking all his money out of the bank
7. is selling his car
8. _____

C Get Together

Work with several other students in your class to come up with a list of suggestions for each of the problems below. Give yourselves three minutes to brainstorm each of the questions. Come up with as many suggestions as you can. Have one student in your group write down all the suggestions. And remember, don't judge your ideas now. That might make you freeze up.

1. Think of a paper cup. How could you use a paper cup other than to drink from? Think of several possible uses for the paper cup.
2. You have to entertain a group of children for an hour. But all you have is a box full of paper cups. How could you use them?
3. Imagine that the paper cup is ten times larger. How might you use it now? What if it's one-tenth its size? If the cup is made of stone, how could you use it?

D Interact

Work with a partner to come up with answers to these questions.

1. Eating the leaves of the leucaena tree affects some animals in an unusual way— their hair begins to fall out. How might this be useful? Who might use this information?
2. The spiderwort flower turns pink when there is a lot of radiation nearby. How could we use these flowers?
3. The armadillo is the only animal other than humans that gets Hansen's disease, a serious disease, also called leprosy. What might humans learn from studying the armadillo?

4. The Basenji dog of Africa does not bark. In what situations could this type of dog be useful?

5. The fastest bird in the world is the swift. It can fly at a speed of 200 miles per hour. Who might be able to get useful information from studying the swift?

Boy, is that bird swift!

4 Remember

Verb Tenses

Rule	Example
Present Tense	In brainstorming, you **write down** every idea that comes into your head. **Are** you a creative person?
Present Perfect Tense	She **has found** a solution to the problem. **Has** he **made** a decision about the job yet?
Past Tense	Tabatha Babbett **came up** with the idea for the circular saw. When **did** Eli Whitney **invent** the cotton gin?

Practice

Complete these sentences with an appropriate tense of the verb.

1. Wang Yani (be) _____ a painter from the People's Republic of China. However, she is no ordinary painter of pictures. She (have) _____ exhibitions of her work since she was four years old.

2. The sixteen-year-old Yani (never/take) _____ art classes at school. However, her father (be) _____ a painter and he (encourage) _____ her since she started painting. When Yani was very young, she (love) _____ to watch him work in his studio. He also (take) _____ her to the zoo to watch the animals, and as soon as she (be) _____ able to hold a brush, she began painting pictures of animals.

3. When Yani was four years old, an art teacher (send) _____ some of her paintings to a well-known artist. He (get) _____ excited when he saw the pictures and wanted to see more of them.

4. When she paints, Yani (like) _____ to listen to the music of Beethoven. She often (paint) _____ in front of a large group of people, but this doesn't bother her. She (be) _____ able to concentrate on her work and to ignore everything else.

5 Pronunciation

/č/ /ǰ/

Repeat these words.

1. church	4. natural	7. catch
2. chicken	5. agricultural	8. patch
3. child	6. statue	9. beach

Repeat these words.

1. jam	5. digest	8. edge
2. giant	6. congestion	9. cage
3. jump	7. college	10. orange
4. jeans		

Now repeat these contrasting words.

1. chest	jest
2. cheer	jeer
3. chin	gin
4. chain	Jane

Repeat these sentences.

1. There's a picture of a child.
2. There's a picture of a child on this page.
3. George is wearing jeans.
4. George is wearing patched jeans.
5. I'd like a ham and cheese sandwich, please.
6. I'd like just a ham and cheese sandwich and orange juice, please.

6 Writing

Get a pencil and a piece of paper ready. You are going to hear some music. As you listen to the music, write down your thoughts about the mood and setting.

> *Example:* It's night time. People are walking down a street. Now they are walking faster and faster. They are throwing things in the air and dancing...

7 Listening

As you listen to the tape, fill in the blanks with the correct words. Then, answer the question at the end of the paragraph.

Adlai E. Stevenson was vice-president from 1893 to 1897.

It is the year 1892 and Adlai E. Stevenson _____ a candidate for the vice-presidency in the United States. Like most of the candidates, he _____ around the country in a train giving speeches. At each town, the train _____ and Stevenson gives a speech. In one area in the northwest part of the country, people _____ very concerned about the naming of a certain mountain. Some people want _____ it Mt. Tacoma. Others want to call it Mt. Rainier. Stevenson _____ give his opinion, but he doesn't want to make anyone angry. "If I say that I like the name Mt. Tacoma, all of the Mt. Rainier people _____ angry. And if I _____ that I like the name Mt. Rainier, none of the Mt. Tacoma people will vote for me. But there _____ some way I can avoid giving my opinion." What do you think Stevenson does?

Mistaken Identity

Never be afraid of making a mistake. Mistakes are often one step in the direction of a solution. Look at the case of Charles Kettering.

Charles Kettering was a great problem solver. During his lifetime, he invented more things than any other American except Thomas Edison. In 1926 Kettering was trying to find ways to improve the automobile. Back then, cars had a lot of problems, so Kettering was a pretty busy man. One problem that really interested Kettering was something called engine "knock." Kettering knew the cause of knock— it took too long for the gasoline to burn up inside the engine— but he didn't know how to get rid of it. He also knew that it was important to solve the problem because knock made the engine inefficient.

Kettering was a pretty good problem solver and he spent a lot of time wondering how to get rid of knock. "If I make the gasoline burn earlier," he thought to himself, "the knocking will stop." But what could make it burn earlier?

Kettering kept thinking about the word *earlier*. He looked around for things that happen early. Suddenly he remembered a plant called the trailing arbutus which blooms earlier than

Charles Kettering

other plants. While studying the plant, he became curious about its unusual red leaves. "It just might be the red in the leaves that makes the plant bloom early," he said to himself. "Maybe if I make the gasoline in the engine red, it will begin to burn earlier."

Kettering looked around his workshop for something to make the gasoline red. There wasn't any red dye, but he did find some red iodine. He added some to the gasoline and to his surprise and delight, the engine stopped knocking.

A few days later, Kettering decided to check his theory. This time he went out and bought some red dye to add to the gasoline. What happened? With the red dye, the engine continued to knock. So much for that idea, thought Kettering. Something in the iodine stopped the engine from knocking but it wasn't the redness. Kettering had his solution, but he had found it by mistake.

A Comprehension and Discussion

1. What does this story teach about problem solving?
2. What problem solving method did Kettering use to solve his problem?
3. Why did Kettering put red dye in the engine?
4. How did Kettering find out that his theory was wrong?
5. What do you think Kettering tried to do next?

B Vocabulary in Context

Look back at the reading to find words that match the definitions below. Write the word on your paper.

1. In the first paragraph, find a word that means *the answer to a problem.*

2. In the second paragraph, find a word that means *to make better.*

3. In the second paragraph, find a word that means *doesn't work well.*

4. In the fourth paragraph, find a word that means *to come into flower.*

5. In the fourth paragraph, find a word that means *to take place.*

6. In the fifth paragraph, find a word that means *pleasure.*

9 Get Together

Work with your classmates to make a list of categories like "things that start early," "red things," "round things." Then follow your instructor's directions.

Now look at the quotations below. Each says something about creativity. Work with a group of students. Read each quotation and decide if you agree or disagree with the idea. Be prepared to explain why.

> Every act of creation is first of all an act of destruction.
> — *Spanish painter Pablo Picasso*
>
> Nothing is more dangerous than an idea when it is the only one you have.
> — *French philosopher Emile Chartier*
>
> Discovery consists of looking at the same thing as everyone else and thinking something different.
> — *Nobel Prize winning physician Albert Szent-Györgyi*
>
> The way to succeed is to double your failure rate.
> — *IBM founder Thomas J. Watson*

UNIT 4 VOCABULARY

Nouns
action
analogy
brainstorm
combination
connection
expert
invention
judge
judgment
method
mistake
mood
problem

product
similarity
solution
substitute
technique

Verbs
act
bloom
combine
connect
contain
delight
evaluate

happen
imagine
improve
invent
relax
solve
stick

Adjectives
creative
curious
efficient
humorous
inefficient

original
playful
related
similar

Expressions
get rid of
make sense

Phrasal verbs
come up (with)
give up

COMMUNICATION
Expressing needs • Discussing qualifications • Discussing pros and cons of
particular occupations • Expressing
probability • Expressing and justifying
opinions

GRAMMAR
Expressing need: *must, have to, have got
to* • Negative form of *must* and *have to*
• Expressing probability: *must* • Gerunds
and infinitives (Review)

Are You Qualified?

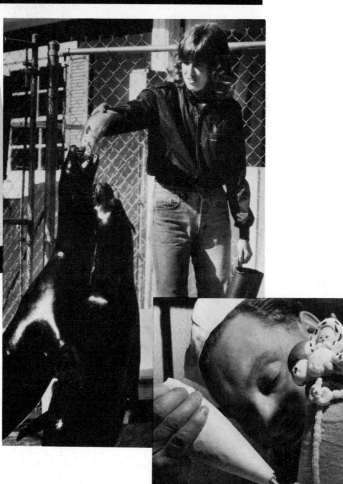

Teaching, running a
business, and taking
care of sick people are
three familiar profes-
sions. The pictures on
this page show people
in less familiar profes-
sions. Can you guess
what their jobs are?
What qualifications
does a person need for
each of these jobs?

Off into Space

The first astronaut team.

Wanted: pilots and engineers. **Must be able to get along with other people. Must be good at performing routine tasks.** You might think this is an advertisement for a job at an airport or in the airplane industry. Actually, it's a job advertisement for astronauts.

When the U.S. space program got going in the 1950s, NASA, the National Aeronautics and Space Administration, began searching for its first team of astronauts. Each of the people on the team had to be in perfect physical shape because no one knew how space travel would affect the body. If a person were in excellent shape, he or she would have a better chance at surviving. Because the astronauts might have to act quickly in an emergency, they also had to be graduates of a test-pilot school. They also had to be shorter than 5'11" (five feet, eleven inches, or 180cm). A taller astronaut would not fit inside the space capsule. Beyond that, the most important qualification was courage. No one was sure the rockets would work.

In recent years the astronaut selection boards have started looking for a new type of person to send into space. Many of today's astronauts work aboard the earth-orbiting space shuttle. They have to launch new satellites into orbit, fix broken satellites, and perform many types of scientific experiments. While each person must have special qualifications, he or she must also be able to work well with other people. Working in space is now a team effort.

There are two categories of astronauts on board today's space shuttle: pilots and mission specialists. Candidates for pilots' positions must have thousands of hours of experience as pilots. They must also have an advanced degree, that is, a degree beyond the bachelor's degree level. Mission specialists perform the "tasks" on space flights. While they do not actually fly the spacecraft, most have a pilot's license. Mission specialists don't have to have a Ph.D.; most candidates, however, have master's degrees in engineering, mathematics, or some field of science. They must also have at least three years of working experience in their field of study.

Many men and women have already flown aboard the shuttle. They have come from the United States, West Germany, Canada, France, Mexico, The Netherlands, and Saudi Arabia. More people will go up in the future. Would you be interested?

In the cargo bay of a space shuttle, two astronauts repair a "captured" satellite.

A Comprehension and Discussion

1. Have the qualifications for becoming an astronaut changed?
2. What are some things that people on the space shuttle have to do?
3. What qualifications must you have to become an astronaut today?
4. What is the difference between a mission specialist and a shuttle pilot?
5. How many space launches have you seen? What do you remember about them?

B Vocabulary

Match each word with the correct definition.

_____ 1. candidate
_____ 2. survive
_____ 3. task
_____ 4. launch
_____ 5. orbit
_____ 6. satellite
_____ 7. shuttle
_____ 8. master's degree
_____ 9. bachelor's degree
_____ 10. Ph.D.

a. go in a circle around something
b. an object that goes around a larger object
c. job or duty
d. the title or rank given after completion of the first four years of university
e. the title given after completion of 1 to 2 years of advanced study in a university
f. the highest title given by a university; usually requires a minimum of 4 years of advanced study
g. set in motion
h. a transport system that goes back and forth between two places
i. remain alive
j. someone who is seeking a position

C Vocabulary in Context

The noun and verb forms of several words are given below. Choose the correct word for each of the sentences below. Make any necessary changes in the form of the verb.

1. *qualifications, qualify*
   a. What _____ do you have to have to get that job?
   b. Do you think I will _____ to become a pilot?
2. *advancement, advance*
   a. It will be difficult _____ if you don't have a university degree.
   b. His _____ to the top of the company took many years.
3. *performance, perform*
   a. They had to _____ many routine tasks.
   b. Her _____ during the flight was perfect.
4. *orbit, to orbit*
   a. The moon _____ the Earth.
   b. The moon's _____ around the Earth is elliptical.
5. *experience, to experience*
   a. Shuttle pilots need thousands of hours of _____.
   b. People from many countries have _____ space flight.
6. *graduate, to graduate*
   a. She _____ from the university in 1980.
   b. You must be a university _____ to enter the space program.
7. *specialist, specialize*
   a. He is a language _____.
   b. Her business _____ in underwater research.

8. *advertisement, advertise*
   a. It costs a lot of money to _____ on TV.
   b. Did you see the _____ for the new restaurant downtown?

2 Focus on Grammar

Expressing Need: Must, Have to, Have Got to
must + the simple form of the verb
have (has) to + the simple form of the verb

Rule	Example
1. *Must* and *have to* indicate that an action or condition is necessary in the present. Use *must* to show a stronger sense of necessity. Use *have to* to describe things that are necessary to do in daily life.	a. An astronaut **must** be in good physical shape. b. People **must** obey the laws. c. You **have to** stop at a stop sign. d. I **have to** get up early tomorrow. e. He **has to** pick up his sister. f. I **have to** stay home and study.
2. In speaking, people sometimes use *have got to* instead of *have to*.	a. I**'ve really got to** leave now. It's late. b. They**'ve got to** buy a new car. Their old car doesn't run anymore.
3. To express necessity in the past, use *had to* + the simple form of the verb.	a. The first astronauts **had to** have courage. b. When the business closed, she **had to** find a new job.

A Practice

Use *must, have (has) to,* or *had to* in the following sentences. Some items have more than one correct answer.

1. To become an astronaut today, you ___*have to*___ have a background in science or engineering.
2. All astronauts _____ be in good physical shape.
3. The first astronauts _____ have plenty of courage. No one was sure that space travel was possible.
4. John Glenn, the first American to orbit Earth, had trouble with the automatic controls on his spacecraft. He _____ control the spacecraft manually.
5. The first astronauts _____ be under the age of 40.

6. When the first men came back from the moon, they _____ stay away from other people. They _____ live in a special building for three weeks.
7. Today, not all crew members of the space shuttle _____ have a pilot's license.
8. Engineers _____ find a way to prevent the space capsule from burning up when it reentered earth's atmosphere.
9. Because they live in a weightless environment, astronauts _____ learn how to float in space.
10. To go into orbit, a satellite _____ reach a speed of 7.8 kilometers per second.

3 Focus on Grammar

Negative Form of Must and Have to
must not + verb

Rule	Example
1. Use *must not* to describe something that is not allowed, or to say that it is very important *not* to do something.	a. You **must not** drink and drive. b. Astronauts **must not** be overweight. c. If the light is red, you **must not** move ahead.
2. Use *don't/doesn't have to* to say that it is not necessary to do something.	a. A person **doesn't have to** have an advanced degree to get a job in some fields. b. I **don't have to** get up until 8 tomorrow because it is a holiday.

A Practice

Fill in the blanks with *must not* or *don't (doesn't) have to*.

1. Astronauts _don't have to_ have a Ph.D.
2. When flying in space, astronauts _____ leave the spacecraft without a special suit.
3. Even while they are living in the spacecraft, astronauts _____ forget to exercise.
4. Astronauts _____ have beds; they can sleep in the air.
5. Astronauts on the space shuttle _____ wear shoes because they float instead of walk.
6. Pilots _____ talk a lot on the radio; the radio is for important communications only.

7. Astronauts on the space shuttle _____ wear spacesuits; they can wear regular clothes.
8. Mission specialists _____ have a pilot's license because they don't fly the spacecraft.
9. Astronauts _____ forget to close doors and drawers inside the shuttle. If they do, things just float away.
10. You _____ be an American to fly on the space shuttle.

B Interact

Read the job descriptions below. Then decide if the statements that follow are true or false.

Scientific and Technical Occupations

Occupation	Type of Work	Training and Qualifications
Aerospace Engineers	Most aerospace engineers work for the aircraft and parts industry.	A bachelor's degree in engineering is required for most beginning jobs. Graduate study is becoming increasingly important for advancement.
Biomedical Engineers	Most biomedical engineers teach and do research in universities. Some work for federal and state agencies or for private industry.	A bachelor's degree in engineering is required for most beginning jobs. Biomedical engineers need some background in mechanical, electrical, industrial, or chemical engineering.
Meteorologists	The National Oceanic and Atmospheric Administration, private industry, and universities all employ meteorologists.	A college degree in meteorology or a related science is necessary. A graduate degree is necessary for research and university teaching jobs.
Oceanographers	About half of all oceanographers teach or do research at universities. A fourth work for federal agencies. The rest work for other government agencies or for private industry.	A college education is necessary. Most beginning positions require a bachelor's degree in oceanography, biology, earth science, mathematics, or engineering. For many advanced positions, however, an advanced degree is necessary.

Write T if the sentence is true. Write F if the sentence is false.

_____ 1. You don't have to have a college degree to become a biomedical engineer.

_____ 2. You must have an advanced degree to be an aerospace engineer.

_____ 3. If you become an oceanographer, you will have to work at a university.

_____ 4. To get a job in oceanography, you must have a bachelor's degree.

_____ 5. You don't have to have an advanced degree to teach meteorology at a university.

Now use the chart to write five true or false statements of your own. Then read your sentences to your classmates, and have them tell you if each statement is true or false.

C | Interact

Practice this dialogue with a partner.

A: Did I tell you? I'm thinking of becoming <u>a chef</u>.

B: <u>A chef</u>! If you become <u>a chef</u>, you'll have to <u>cook all day in a hot kitchen</u>!

A: <u>Chefs</u> don't have to <u>cook all day</u>. They also get to <u>taste the food</u>.

A: Did I tell you? I'm thinking of becoming _____.

B: _____! If you become _____, you'll have to _____!

A: _____ don't have to _____. They also get to _____.

1. doctor
2. astronomer
3. veterinarian
4. teacher
5. computer programmer
6. photographer
7. oceanographer
8. reporter
9. farmer
10. _____

4 Focus on Grammar

Expressing Probability: Must
must + the simple form of the verb

Rule	Example
You can also use *must* and *must not* to describe what you think is true based on the information that you have.	a. No one answered the phone. My husband **must not** be home yet. b. He didn't go to work yesterday because he felt sick. But he did go to work today. He **must** be feeling better today.

A Practice

Decide what you think is probably true based on the information given in the sentences below. Use *must* or *must not* in your sentences.

1. She didn't answer the telephone. <u>She must not be at home.</u>
2. He went to sleep very early. _____
3. Her phone has been busy for an hour. _____
4. The trees outside are really moving back and forth.
   _____
5. This restaurant is very crowded. _____
6. Why are we the only people in this movie theater?
   _____
7. It's very dark outside tonight. _____
8. His plane left for Italy seven hours ago. _____
9. He hasn't eaten anything for days. _____
10. Everyone wants to take this course. _____
11. No one came to the party. _____
12. I can't find my wallet. _____

B Interact

With a partner, practice this dialogue.

A: He must really be <u>tired</u>.
B: Why do you say that?

A: Didn't you know? He <u>ran in a 20 kilometer race this morning</u>.
B: You're right. He must be <u>tired</u>!

A: He must really be _____.
B: Why do you say that?

A: Didn't you know? He just _____.
B: You're right. He must be _____!

1. sleepy
2. happy
3. angry
4. sore
5. thankful
6. courageous
7. rich
8. surprised
9. inefficient
10. _____

5 Remember

Gerunds and Infinitives (Review)
verb + ing; to + verb

Rule	Example
Gerunds often follow these verbs and expressions: *appreciate, avoid, delay, deny, discuss, dislike, enjoy, finish, mind, miss, practice, quit, regret, stop, try, have trouble, be afraid of, become accustomed to, get used to, be careful about, be excited about, be good at, be interested in, look forward to, be nervous about, talk about, get tired of, think about, spend time.*	a. She enjoys flying.
Infinitives often follow these verbs: *afford, agree, ask, decide, demand, expect, forget, hope, learn, need, plan, promise, refuse, seem, wait, want, wish.*	b. He expects to work outdoors.
Infinitives or Gerunds may follow these verbs: *begin, can't stand, continue, hate, like, love, prefer, start, try.*	c. He can't stand to look for a job. d. She can't stand looking for a new job.

A Practice

Fill in the blanks with a gerund or infinitive.

Clown

Would you be interested in (work) ___working___ for the circus? If so, you might think about (go) _____ to Ringling Brothers Barnum and Bailey's clown training school in Florida. Every year the circus officials hire 30 students from the school (work) _____ as clowns.

Forest Fire Lookout

Do you enjoy (live) _____ alone? The U.S. Forest Service hires people (work) _____ in forest lookout towers in the national parks. These people need (watch) _____ for signs of fire. In past years, the Forest Service encouraged newlywed couples (apply) _____ for this job. The Forest Service thought newlywed couples would like (live) _____ together in a lookout tower.

Street Vendor

Do you dislike (work) _____ indoors? Do you like to spend time (watch) _____ people on the street? Can you persuade people (buy) _____ things? If so, you might want (become) _____ a street vendor. In the U.S. you need (have) _____ a license to sell things on the street, but it's not very expensive to get the license.

6 Pronunciation

/s/ /š/ /ž/

Repeat these words.

1. second
2. sufficient
3. ceiling
4. passenger
5. muscle

6. listen
7. place
8. pass
9. base

Now repeat these words.

1. she
2. should
3. chauffeur
4. insure
5. machine

6. condition
7. brush
8. push
9. flash

Repeat these words.

1. measure
2. leisure
3. pleasure

4. collision
5. treasure
6. garage

Now repeat these contrasting words.

1. see   she
2. sew   show
3. sell   shell
4. puss   push

5. thresher   measure
6. glacier   glazier
7. fission   vision

Repeat these sentences.

1. Were they sure of the location of the ship?
2. A chaffeur should be certain that the car's in excellent condition.
3. A chaffeur should be certain that the car's in the garage.
4. She should show you the old machine.
5. She should show you how to sew on the old machine.

10...9...8...7...6...5...4...3...2...1

How would you like to go up in the space shuttle? It's not an impossibility. Many people have already taken the trip and more will go up in the future. You will have to make some adjustments if you go up, because living in space is a bit different from living on earth. But no one so far has had trouble making the changes.

What do you wear in space?

Once you are in space, you don't have to wear special clothing— you can dress just as you do on Earth. However, you do have to have plenty of big pockets in your clothing. Books, spoons, tools, and other things you use must go in your pocket; otherwise, they will float away. Shoes are unnecessary because you don't have to walk on the floor. You can just float in space.

How do you move around?

You have to get used to being weightless in space. Sally Ride described her first day in space like this:

> I had to learn how to move around. I started out trying to "swim" through the air, but that didn't work at all; air isn't dense, the way water is, and I felt silly dog-paddling in the air, going nowhere. Before long I discovered that I had to push off from the walls if I wanted to get across the room. At first I would push off a little too hard and crash into the opposite wall, but I soon learned to wind my way around with very gentle pushes.

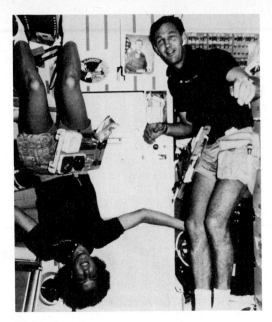

Eating in space

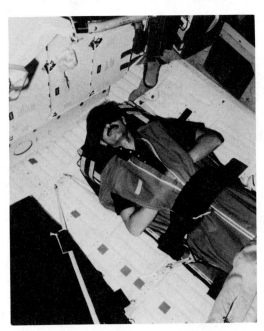

Sleeping in space

What do you eat?

Eating is not easy aboard the space-craft. If you spill coffee or juice, it just floats around the cabin in balls. Salt is impossible to use in space. The grains of salt won't come out of the salt shaker. Instead, you have to use salt and pepper in liquid form. Astronauts now know that they must not take chili into space. On one flight, containers of food with chili exploded when the astronauts opened them. Before the flight, all food must be precooked, dehydrated, and packaged. To return moisture to the food, you have to use a needle to put water into the packages. Foods like peanut butter, puddings, or sauces are the easiest to eat because they stick to your spoon. Other food just floats off your spoon.

How do you keep clean?

Keeping clean can be a problem. Toilets have special suction pumps which pull the waste away. There is no sink or shower in the space shuttle because water would just float away in little balls around the cabin. Instead, you must use a special water gun. Toothpaste is digestible, so you can swallow it. Remember, there's no place to spit.

How do you sleep?

You don't have to have a bed on the shuttle. You can tie a special sleeping bag to the wall of the spacecraft and sleep there. Or you can just float around in the cabin while you are sleeping. You might float into some-thing, but you will never have to worry about falling out of bed.

Comprehension and Discussion 🔲

1. What routine things are more difficult to do in space?
2. Why don't you have to wear shoes in the space shuttle?
3. What problems did Sally Ride have moving in space?
4. Why must you swallow the toothpaste?
5. What would you like or dislike about living in space?

Decide if the following sentences are true or false.

6. Astronauts on the shuttle need not wear shoes.   T   F
7. In space, you have to use salt in liquid form.   T   F
8. Astronauts have to sleep in beds.   T   F
9. Things will float away if they are not secured.   T   F
10. Food on the shuttle must not be dehydrated.   T   F

B **Vocabulary in Context**

Fill in the blanks with the correct word. Use each word only once.

Verbs	Adjectives
float	gentle
crash	dense
contain	dehydrated
swallow	sticky
spit	digestible

1. All of those buckets _____ water.
2. On Earth, people cannot _____ in the air; they can only do this on water.
3. Gases are less _____ than liquids.
4. It's important to chew your food well before you _____ it.
5. Your body can break down and use _____ food.
6. If you go for too long without drinking liquids, you will feel _____.
7. He wanted to _____ out the water because it tasted bad.
8. He has to learn to be _____. He hurt my fingers when we shook hands.
9. Chewing gum is very _____; it's very difficult to remove from clothing.
10. Motorcyclists wear special helmets to protect their heads in case they _____ into something.

8 Writing

Interview a friend or relative about her or his job. Find out what kinds of routine tasks the person does. Find out the qualifications a person must have in order to do this job. Report your findings in writing without identifying the job. Read your report to the class and see if they can name the job.

9 Listening

Study the job application below. Then listen to the conversation. You will hear an employer interviewing an applicant for a job in the Burgerland restaurant. Use the information from the interview to complete the form below. You will hear the conversation twice.

BurgerLand

BurgerLand   Application for Employment
54 West Drive

Please complete all applicable areas of the application.

Name: _____ HARRIS _____ P. _____
            Last   First   Middle Initial

Address: _22 Prince Street_ _Auburn,_   _Michigan_ _____
              Street   City   State

Telephone: _682-8830_____

Position Applied For: _cashier_____

Are you looking for   Educational Information
full time work? _____

	School	No. of Years Completed	Graduation (Yes) (No)
Are you looking for part time work? _____			
Have you ever worked here before? _____	Elementary	8	Yes
Have you ever done this type of work? _____			
How old are you? _20_____	High School	4	
Previous employer: _____	College		

---

10 │ Get Together

Work with several of your classmates to do the following:

A. Choose a job, any kind of job.
B. Make a list of questions to ask someone who comes to interview for the job.
C. With the students in your group, role-play an interview that shows either what you must do or must not do at an interview. Perform your sample interview for the rest of the class. Have them identify what was good or bad about the interview.

UNIT 5 VOCABULARY

Nouns			
advancement	moisture	advertise	swallow
advertisement	performance	contain	survive
astronaut	Ph.D.	crash	
bachelor's degree	pocket	dress	*Adjectives*
candidate	program	experience	dehydrated
capsule	qualification	explode	dense
category	satellite	fit	digestible
courage	shape	fix	excellent
degree	shuttle	float	gentle
effort	space	launch	opposite
emergency	specialist	orbit	perfect
engineer	team	perform	physical
experience	task	qualify	recent
graduate		search	routine
license	*Verbs*	specialize	sticky
master's degree	adjust	spit	sure
	advance	stick	weightless

UNIT 6

COMMUNICATION
Suggesting doing something
• Expressing advisability • Giving advice
or a warning • Stating a supposition to
elicit agreement/disagreement

GRAMMAR
Present unreal conditional statements
• Expressing obligation and expectation:
be supposed to • Expressing advisabil-
ity: *should, ought to, had better*
• Comparatives of change

Rules and Laws

NO TRESPASSING

...LIC SERVICE

STATE LAW
REQUIRES PROOF OF AGE!
MINORS UNDER
21
WILL NOT BE SERVED
ALCOHOLIC BEVERAGES

SPEED LIMIT 30
TPD

YIELD

NO PARKING ANY TIME

RIGHT LANE FOR EXIT ONLY

What laws are the same everywhere in the world? What laws are different? If you saw someone breaking the law, what would you do? Give an example. Each of the signs on this page illustrates a rule or law. Where might you see these signs? What should or shouldn't you do in each situation?

1 Reading 🔈

There Ought to Be a Law

Prereading Exercise

This unit uses a number of legal terms. Some of these words are *italicized* in the sentences below. Read each sentence and match it with the definition in the column on the right that is closest in meaning to the *italicized* word.

_____ 1. The police *arrested* him for driving dangerously.

_____ 2. Do you know the *penalty* for driving too fast?

_____ 3. In most U.S. states, you can get a driver's *license* when you are 16 years old.

_____ 4. The judge *sentenced* the thief to five years in jail.

_____ 5. The jury decided that he was *guilty*.

_____ 6. They spent 17 weeks writing the U.S. *Constitution*.

_____ 7. Twenty-six *amendments* have been made to the U.S. Constitution.

_____ 8. My brother is a *lawyer* who specializes in tax law.

_____ 9. Many states have passed *tough* new laws.

a. punishment
b. took to jail
c. formal changes
d. legal permission to do something
e. responsible for breaking a law
f. hard; strict
g. a person who studies the law and advises people in court
h. the basic laws for governing a state or country
i. decided on a penalty

What would you do if a drunk driver killed someone in your family? Candy Lightner had to answer that question in 1980 when a car ran into and killed her daughter. The driver of the car was not supposed to be on the road— he had had too much to drink. And he had a long record of arrests for drunk driving.

Lightner was devastated by the accident. Then she learned that the driver might not go to jail. He would probably only lose his license for a while. Lightner couldn't believe it. The laws were supposed to protect innocent people. The penalties for drunk driving were supposed to discourage people from driving while intoxicated. But losing your license for a short time was not a very tough penalty.

On the eve of her daughter's funeral, Lightner decided to start an organization to stop drunk drivers. She didn't have a plan or a goal, but she was determined to get publicity and tougher penalties. If people thought more about the dangers, fewer people would drink and drive. And if the penalties were tougher, people would think twice before drinking and driving.

Some of Lightner's friends thought that she should just forget about it. You couldn't change the laws. But Lightner wasn't going to give up. First she went to California Governor Jerry Brown to get his help. She was persistent. She went to his office every day until Brown finally appointed a group of people to study the problem. Lightner's organization, Mothers Against Drunk Driving (MADD), had the go-ahead.

Candy Lightner and her organization have made a difference. Since 1980 every state has passed tougher penalties for driving while intoxicated (DWI). Today if the police arrested you for drunk driving, you could lose your license for one year.

And if it were your second offense, you could lose your license for up to two years. And that is what would happen if no one were hurt. If you killed someone while drinking and driving, you would face a mandatory jail sentence.

Most states are also trying to keep drunk drivers off the road. The police are stopping more drivers to give alcohol tests. Some states are experimenting with a device that should prevent drunk drivers from starting their cars. The device has a built-in microprocessor that is supposed to pick up alcohol on the driver's breath. This doesn't solve drinking problems, but it does keep drunk drivers off the roads.

MADD now has more than one million members. Lightner still makes speeches around the country, talks to lawmakers, and gets attention for the problem. As Lightner says, "We are changing the way people think about drinking and driving. But more than that, we have caused people to change their behavior, and that is saving lives."

Mothers Against Drunk Driving

A Comprehension and Discussion

1. Why do you think some people drink and drive even though it is dangerous?
2. What do you think is the best way to stop people from drinking and driving?
3. How would you describe Candy Lightner?
4. How has the organization MADD helped to prevent drunk driving?
5. Do you think the built-in microprocessor will work? Why or why not?
6. Does the reading tell you what happened to the driver of the car that killed Lightner's daughter?
7. What does the acronym MADD stand for?

B Vocabulary in Context

Read the sentences in the column on the left. Match each sentence with the word or phrase in the column on the right that is closest in meaning to the *italicized* word or phrase.

_____ 1. The laws are supposed to protect *innocent* people.

_____ 2. His car *ran into* a tree.

_____ 3. He would only lose his license for *a while*.

_____ 4. She was very *persistent*. She went to the governor's office every day.

_____ 5. In some states the penalty is a *mandatory* jail sentence.

_____ 6. Some states are *experimenting with* a built-in microprocessor.

_____ 7. It won't *solve* drinking problems.

a. a short time
b. required
c. not guilty
d. testing
e. find an answer; get rid of
f. refusing to give up; insistent
g. hit; collided with

2 Focus on Grammar

Present Unreal Conditional Statements
If + past tense verb: unreal conditional

Rule	Example
1. Use the present unreal conditional to talk about a condition that is untrue in the present.	a. If I knew the answer, I would tell you. *(I don't know the answer. Therefore, I cannot tell you the answer.)* b. If I weren't sick, I would go to work. *(I am sick. Therefore, I am not going to work.)*

(continued)

Present Unreal Conditional Statements (continued)

Rule	Example
	if clause *result clause*
2. A present unreal conditional statement has an *if* clause and a *result* clause.	a. If you were in trouble, I would help.
3. To form the present unreal conditional, use the past form of the verb in the *if* clause (to show present time). Use *would* + the simple form of the verb in the *result* clause (to show definite intention).	a. If I **had** a million dollars, I **would** give half to you. b. If I **didn't know** the answer, I **would** ask you. c. What **would** you do if someone **stole** your car?
4. To show ability or possibility instead of intention, use *could* or *might* + the simple form of the verb in the result clause.	a. If my car broke down, I **could take** the bus. b. If you **broke** the law, you **might go** to jail.
5. The verb *be* has a special form in the present unreal conditional. Use *were* in all persons.	a. If I **were** you, I would get a new job. b. If he **were** sick, he would call. c. If the penalties **were** tougher, fewer people would drink and drive.

A **Practice**

Complete the following sentences. Use the past form of the verb in the *if* clause. Use *would* + the simple form of the verb in the result clause.

1. I don't have a lot of money.
   If I ___*had*___ a lot of money, I ___*would give it all to you*___.
2. I know her telephone number.
   If I ___*didn't know*___ her telephone number, I ___*would ask her friends for it*___.
3. I'm tired today.
   If I _____ tired today, I _____.
4. Many people break the law.
   If people _____, there _____.
5. She doesn't have a driver's license.
   If she _____, she _____.
6. Every country has laws.
   If a country _____ laws, _____.
7. She is not very persistent.
   If she _____ more persistent, she _____.

8. Many people still drink and drive.
   If they _____, there _____.
9. Many people don't think about the dangers of drinking and driving.
   If they _____ about the dangers, they _____.
10. I am not a lawyer.
   If I _____ a lawyer, I _____.

B Practice

Describe two things that you could do in each of these situations. Use *could* or *might* to complete the result clause.

Example: If I needed money, _I could sell my car or get a loan from the bank_.

1. If I didn't like the rules in school, _____.
2. If my car broke down on the highway, _____.
3. If I lost my wallet, _____.
4. If I saw someone stealing something, _____.
5. If I wanted to cheer up a friend, _____.
6. If I had a backache, _____.
7. If I wanted to get someone's phone number, _____.
8. If I lived near the ocean, _____.
9. If I wanted to learn about the laws in another country,
   _____.
10. If I wanted to travel across the country, _____.
11. If I didn't understand your question, _____.
12. If I didn't know the answer to your question, _____.

C Interact

Laws tells us how to act in some situations. Custom and common sense tell us what to do in other situations. With a partner, practice this dialogue.

A: What would you do if <u>a stranger gave you an expensive gift</u>?
B: If <u>a stranger gave me an expensive gift, I would give it back</u>.

A: What would you do if _____?
B: If _____, I _____.

1. you received a letter addressed to somebody else
2. you hated what your host served at dinner
3. you lost the heel to your shoe on the way to a job interview
4. you forgot to go to a dinner party at your boss' house
5. you took the wrong coat from a restaurant coatrack by mistake
6. your guests got into a big argument over dinner
7. your good friend refused to talk to you anymore
8. you found one hundred dollars on the street
9. a stranger accused you of stealing in a store
10. _____

D Practice

In some very special situations you might have to break a law, rule, or social custom. Work with a small group of students to think of situations when someone might do the things below. Use *if* in your sentences.

Example: I would break down a door if there were a fire inside.

1. break down a door
2. park in a no-parking area
3. drive above the speed limit
4. break a window
5. push someone to the ground
6. remove something from a stranger's car
7. stop on the highway
8. make a lot of noise in a public place
9. run out of a restaurant
10. wear a bathing suit to dinner
11. refuse to help someone
12. hide someone's car keys

3 Focus on Grammar

Expressing Obligation and Expectation
Be supposed to + verb

Rule	Example
Use the verb *be supposed to* when you want to talk about: • things we should and shouldn't do • things that we are required to do • expectations • things that we expected would happen in the past but did not happen • something that is generally believed to be true Form the expression with *be + supposed to +* the simple form of a verb. For negative statements, use *be + not + supposed to +* the verb.	a. Everyone **is supposed to obey** the laws. b. You **are** not **supposed to drink and drive**. c. Alcohol testing is **supposed to keep** drunk drivers off the road. d. The penalty was **supposed to discourage** people from breaking the law. (It did not.) e. Exercise is **supposed to be** good for you. (*It is believed that exercise is good for* you.)

Practice

Signs tell us what we are supposed to do or not supposed to do on the road. Look at each of the signs on this page. Make sentences with *you're supposed to* or *you're not supposed to*. You can also say *"we're (not) supposed to...."*

Mrs. Tanner had to leave work early, so she left a note for her secretary to tell him what to do.

Paul:

1. Call Mr. Bigelow and make an appointment for Thursday, 10 a.m.
2. Make three copies of the letter to Ms. Esquivel and leave them on my desk.
3. Call Mr. Cook and cancel the appointment for this afternoon.
4. Make a reservation on Midwestern Airline's Cleveland-to-Chicago flight for the morning of June 9.
5. Order ten boxes of envelopes and fifteen boxes of letter paper.
6. Type the letter to Best Industries and leave it on my desk. Don't mail it.

When Mrs. Tanner arrived at work the next day, she found this note from Paul.

Memo

1. I called Mr. Bigelow and made an appointment for Friday at 11.
2. I ordered fifteen boxes of envelopes and ten boxes of letter paper.
3. I made two copies of the letter to Ms. Esquivel.
4. I typed the letter to Best Industries and mailed it.
5. I called Midwestern Airlines and made a reservation on their flight from Cleveland to San Francisco on June 19.
6. I forgot to call Mr. Cook, but I'll call him tomorrow.

Paul

Mrs. Tanner was very angry. Write a paragraph about what you think she said to Paul. Use *be (not) supposed to*.

> *Example:* You were supposed to make an appointment for Thursday at 10 a.m.

C | Interact

Practice this dialogue with a partner.

A: You look upset. What's wrong?
B: I was supposed to <u>pick up my aunt an hour ago</u>, but I forgot.

A: Hmmm. That could be a problem. If I were you, I'd <u>go try to find her. And I'd pick up some flowers on the way</u>.
B: That's a good idea. Thanks.

A: You look upset. What's wrong?
B: I was supposed to _____, but I forgot.

A: Hmmm. That could be a problem. If I were you, I'd _____.
B: That's a good idea. Thanks.

1. go to a job interview this morning
2. meet my boss for dinner
3. put gas in my husband's/wife's car yesterday
4. cook something for a special dinner tonight
5. leave my wife/husband the car keys
6. buy my wife/husband a birthday present
7. go to an important meeting this morning
8. lock the house
9. turn the stove off at home
10. put on a suit for an important meeting this afternoon
11. _____

D | Interact

Some cities and towns in the United States have funny laws. Some of these laws are old laws that no one has bothered to change. Others were made to solve specific problems. Each of the pictures on the next page illustrates an unusual law. Work with your classmates to guess what each law is. Use *supposed to* or *not supposed to*.

> *Example:* You're not supposed to wear a hat in a movie theater in Texas.

Abilene, Texas

New York City

New York City

North Dakota

Pontiac, Michigan

Answers

1. Abilene Texas: You are not supposed to whistle at girls.
2. New York City: You are not supposed to open an umbrella in front of a horse.
3. New York City: You are not supposed to read while walking down the street.
4. North Dakota: You're not supposed to wear a mask on the street.
5. Pontiac, Michigan: Passengers are supposed to sit in the back seat.

4 Focus on Grammar

Expressing Advisability
should/ought to/had better + simple form of verb

Rule	Examples
1. Use *should* or *ought to* + the simple form of a verb to give advice.	a. You **should** slow down. b. You **shouldn't** drive so fast. c. He **ought to** stop for awhile.
2. Use the expression *had better* or *had better not* to offer a warning or to give advice. Although the expression *had better* is in the past tense, it always refers to the present or future. Notice that we usually use the contraction form of *had*: I'd, she'd, we'd, they'd.	a. The speed limit is 55 mph. You**'d better** slow down. b. It's getting cold outside. You**'d better** put on a sweater. c. We**'d better** do something to reduce the number of fatalities on the road.

A Practice

Read each sentence and give a warning or advice using *should, ought to,* or *had better (not)*. Some items have more than one correct answer.

Example: It's raining outside. *You'd better take an umbrella.*

1. The video store closes in ten minutes. _____
2. There's ice on the front steps. _____
3. That cup is cracked. _____
4. There's a stop sign. _____
5. That knife is very sharp. _____
6. There's a police car ahead. _____
7. I smell something burning. _____
8. The brakes on my bike aren't working. _____
9. That wet floor is slippery. _____
10. This is a one-way street. _____

B Interact

Practice this dialogue with a partner.

A: Wait a minute!
B: What's wrong?

A: You're not supposed to <u>turn left here</u>.
B: You're right. I didn't see the sign. I guess I'd better <u>take the next left</u>.

A: Wait a minute!
B: What's wrong?

A: You're not supposed to _____.
B: You're right. I didn't see the sign. I guess I'd better _____.

1. go faster than 55 mph
2. walk on the grass
3. park here
4. smoke in here
5. roller-skate on the sidewalk
6. pick the flowers

7. use that emergency exit
8. take your dog into a restaurant
9. touch the paintings in a museum
10. feed the animals in a zoo
11. _____

C Interact

Remember that *be supposed to* is sometimes used to mean *it is believed that*. Practice this dialogue with a partner.

A: <u>Women are</u> supposed to <u>be more emotional than men</u>.
B: I don't agree. <u>I know many men who are emotional. It depends on the person.</u>

A: _____ supposed to _____.
B: I (don't) agree. _____.

1. Children are supposed to grow taller than their parents.
2. Studying math is supposed to develop a more logical mind.
3. Sea air is supposed to be good for your health.
4. A firm handshake is supposed to be a sign of honesty.
5. Silent people are supposed to be deep thinkers.
6. Tough penalties are supposed to discourage crime.
7. Memorizing things is supposed to improve your "memory power."
8. A restaurant with many cars outside is supposed to be a good place to eat.

9. Eating green apples is supposed to give you a stomachache.
10. Eating garlic is supposed to make you live longer.
11. _____

5 Focus on Grammar

Comparatives of Change
double comparatives joined by and

Rule	Example
Use the comparative form of an adjective + *and* + the same comparative form of the adjective to show that things are continuing to change.	a. Communications are getting **better and better**. b. The questions on the test seem to become **more and more difficult**.

A Practice

Fill in the blanks with the comparative form of each adjective.

1. (tough) The penalties for drunk driving are becoming _tougher and tougher_.
2. (bad) Over the past twenty years, the traffic has gotten _____.
3. (hungry) As the hours passed, my brother got _____.
4. (important) Over the past twenty years, technology has become _____ in banking and industry.
5. (good) The movie got _____ the longer we watched it.
6. (sleepy) I get _____ the later it gets.
7. (difficult) It is getting _____ to remember all the grammar rules.
8. (fast) It seems as if people are driving _____.
9. (low) As we went up the mountain, the temperature get _____.
10. (slow) Time seems to go by _____ the longer you wait.

6 Pronunciation

/1/ /r/

Repeat these words.

1. like	3. little	5. class	7. mobile
2. last	4. welcome	6. collect	8. twelve

Repeat these words.

1. rest	3. raise	5. hurry	7. southern
2. right	4. service	6. improve	8. longer

Repeat these contrasting words.

1. light   right   **4.** Eileen   Irene
2. long   wrong   **5.** file   fire
3. play   pray   **6.** tile   tire

Now repeat these sentences.

1. The original buildings at Children's Hospital were built in 1932.
2. Right now I'm contacting friends in the entertainment world to help.
3. I may stay a little longer to see some of the tennis tournament.

7 **Listening** 🎞

Listen to the conversation between a father and his daughter. Fill in the blanks with the words that you hear.

Mr. Lund: You know you're in trouble. You'd better sit down and explain your _____.

Sarah: Dad, don't be _____ on me. I know I wasn't supposed to take the car. I won't pretend to be _____. But Nikki had to get to the bus station. And you weren't home so I couldn't ask you to take him. I didn't go very far. Honest!

Mr. Lund: That's not the point. If you had a _____, I would let you use the car. But you only have a learner's permit. What would happen if everyone _____ the law? What if people thought they could do anything they wanted to do?

Sarah: I know, I know. We have _____ for a reason. But you can't go to _____ for driving without a license, can you?

Mr. Lund: I really don't know what the _____ is. But you do understand that I'll have to punish you.

Sarah: I figured as much.

Take It To Court

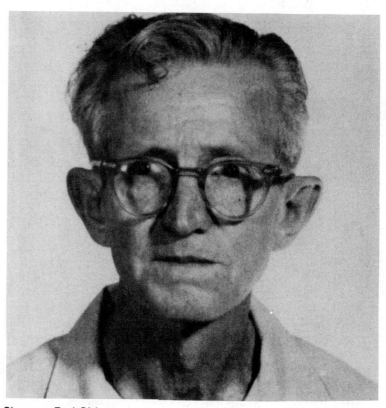

Clarence Earl Gideon

1 If you had to go to court, would you hire a lawyer or try to defend yourself? Most people would hire a lawyer— that is, if they could afford one. But what would you do if you couldn't afford a lawyer?

Until 1963 in the United States, the courts were supposed to provide poor people with a lawyer in cases that might lead to the death penalty. 2 But in other cases, a poor person was supposed to defend himself or herself. One important court case changed that.

Clarence Earl Gideon's problems started when he was a child. His father died when he was only three years old. When his mother remarried, he and his stepfather didn't get along. At the age of 14, Gideon finally ran away from home. Then he started to steal, first clothing from a store, then money. At the age of 18 he was in prison. For the next 24 years, Gideon was in and out of prisons for stealing. But in 1952, things seemed to change for Gideon. He got married, had children, and stayed out of trouble with the law— until 1961.

3

On June 3, 1961, somone broke into the Bay Harbor Poolroom in Panama City, Florida. The thief took some wine and a little change from a cigarette machine and juke box. The police arrested Clarence Earl Gideon. He was 51 years old at the time.

4

Gideon's trial took place on August 4, 1961. When the trial began, the judge asked Gideon,

"Are you ready to go to trial?"

"I am not ready, your Honor," Gideon answered.

"Why aren't you ready?"

"I don't have a lawyer."

"Why don't you have a lawyer? Didn't you know that your case was set for today?"

5

Gideon explained that he could not afford a lawyer, and he asked the judge to appoint one for him. The judge denied his request.

6

Gideon's trial didn't take long. Gideon was supposed to defend himself, but he didn't know what to say. He tried to convince the jury that he was innocent, but they didn't

7

believe him and found him guilty. At the end of the trial, the judge sentenced him to five years in prison, the maximum sentence.

Gideon then decided to convince the Supreme Court to review his case. But how was he supposed to do this without a lawyer's help? Gideon looked up information in the few law books in the prison library. Then he filled out a petition and sent it to the Supreme Court. Although the Supreme Court hears only 10 percent of the petitions sent to it, it decided to review Clarence Gideon's case.

8

The Supreme Court appointed a lawyer, Abe Fortas, to defend Gideon. Fortas built his argument around the 14th Amendment to the U.S. Constitution. This amendment says that everyone is supposed to have equal protection of the laws. Fortas pointed out that if a person did not have a lawyer, he could not get a fair trial. On March 18, 1963, the Supreme Court gave its decision on Gideon's case. It agreed that Gideon had not received a fair trial in Florida. This decision changed the way courts held trials all over the country. After this decision, all states had to provide poor people with lawyers.

9

Gideon's troubles were not over. The Supreme Court decision only allowed him a new trial— this time with a lawyer. On August 5, 1963, Gideon went to the same courtroom and stood before the same judge. But this time he had a lawyer by his side. The new jury listened to both sides and then gave a verdict of not guilty.

10

A | Comprehension and Discussion

1. How would you describe Clarence Earl Gideon?
2. What kind of life did Gideon have? Explain your answer.
3. What trouble did Gideon have with the law before 1961?
4. Why did the police arrest Gideon in 1961?
5. Why didn't Gideon hire a lawyer?
6. What did the Supreme Court decision do for Gideon?
7. How was Gideon's second trial different from his first trial?
8. Why was this Supreme Court case important?

B | Vocabulary in Context

Go back to the reading and find the paragraph indicated below. Find a word in the paragraph that matches the definition given in *italics*.

1. In paragraph #1, find a word that means *be able to pay for.*
   _____

2. In paragraph #2, find a word that means *protect oneself.*
   _____

3. In paragraph #3, find a word that means *jail.*
   _____

4. In paragraph #4, find a word that means *take to jail.*
   _____

5. In paragraph #6, find a word that means *choose a person for a job.*
   _____

6. In paragraph #7, find a word that means *not innocent.*
   _____

7. In paragraph #8, find a word that means *look over again.*
   _____

8. In paragraph #10, find a word that means *a decision by a court.*
   _____

9 New Expressions: Phrasal Verbs

Separable	
point out	*bring to someone's attention*
look up	*look for information in a book*
give up	*quit*
Inseparable	
run away	*leave a place without permission*

Fill in the blanks with a phrasal verb. Use each verb in the correct form. You may use a verb more than once.

1. Candy Lightner refused to _____ the fight for stronger laws.
2. I decided to _____ the date in an encyclopedia. I couldn't find it there so I _____ it _____ in a history book.
3. Her father _____ the weak points in her argument.
4. Gideon was only 14 years old when he _____.
5. He _____ her number _____ in the phone book.
6. He doesn't play soccer anymore. He had to _____ it _____ because he hurt his leg.

10 Writing

If you had an accident while driving, you would have to fill out a form for the insurance company. Study the illustration of the accident on the right side of the form. Some of the form has been filled out. On your paper, write the "Driver's description of accident."

Accident Report Form

Did you see the other car before collision?	YES	NO

Describe position of other car when you first saw it	*The other car drove up behind me.*
Describe position of your car at that same moment	*My car was standing at a stop sign.*

Driver's description of accident *(Must be completed in detail)*	Please illustrate on this diagram how accident occurred

Other car

My car

STOP

11 Get Together

Work in a small group. Decide what you think each of these sayings means. Think of an example to illustrate each saying.

1. An eye for an eye and a tooth for a tooth.
2. The punishment should fit the crime.
3. Punishment is always a two-edged sword.
4. A sensible man does not punish a man because he has done wrong but in order to keep him from doing wrong.

Now, work together to prepare a short description of the drinking and driving laws in your country. Is it illegal to drink before a certain age? At what age can a person legally start to drive? Are there laws against drunken driving in your country? If there are students from different countries in your class, make a chart to compare the laws in each country.

UNIT 6 VOCABULARY

Nouns
accident
amendment
attention
behavior
court
court case
danger
device
funeral
go-ahead
goal
jail
jury
law
lawyer
license

member
offense
organization
penalty
petition
prison
publicity
record
request
(jail) sentence
trial
verdict

Verbs
afford
appoint
arrest

break (a law)
defend
devastate
discourage
experiment
hire
obey
protect
review
solve
steal

Adjectives
built-in
fair
guilty
innocent

mandatory
maximum
persistent
tough

Adverbs
while

Phrasal Verbs
point out
give up
look up
run away
run into

Expressions
think twice

COMMUNICATION
Expressing reservations ▪
Stating alternate outcomes ▪ Saying
goodbye ▪ Talking about past time
sequence

GRAMMAR
Past perfect tense ▪ Past perfect
continuous tense

Newcomers

Since 1900, more than 33 million people have moved to the United States and become citizens. The charts show where these people came from. How has immigration changed over the years? Is the number of immigrants from Europe increasing or decreasing? From Asia?

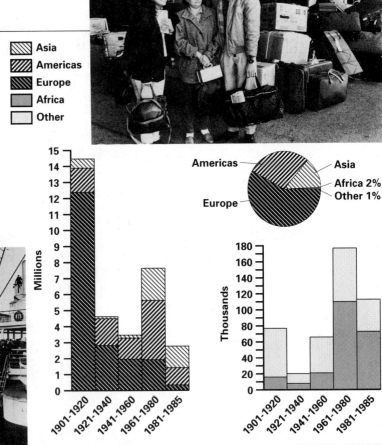

Asia
Americas
Europe
Africa
Other

Millions

15
14
13
12
11
10
9
8
7
6
5
4
3
2
1
0

1901-1920 1921-1940 1941-1960 1961-1980 1981-1985

Americas   Asia
Africa 2%
Other 1%
Europe

Thousands

180
160
140
120
100
80
60
40
20
0

1901-1920 1921-1940 1941-1960 1961-1980 1981-1985

Transplanted Talent

An Wang in 1979 with one of his computers

An Wang came to the United States in 1945. In 1986, he was one of 12 immigrants to receive a Liberty Medal from the President of the United States. Dr. Wang died in 1990.

On his way home from school one day, An Wang found a bird's nest that had fallen from a tree. Inside the nest was a baby sparrow. Wang picked up the nest and took it home with him. He was a little nervous about showing his parents what he had found, so he decided to leave the nest outside for a while. When he finally went outside to get the bird, he found that it had disappeared. He realized then that he had lost the bird because he had not brought it in immediately. "It was my first lesson in the importance of acting rather than hesitating," Wang wrote many years later. It was a lesson that stayed with Wang for his entire life.

When An Wang came to the United States in 1945, he had already lost both of his parents and one sister. He had also survived a civil war in China and somehow, during the upheaval in his country of birth, he had finished his studies at the university. But the troubles he had experienced early in life taught him an important lesson. By the time he left China, he believed that he could try to accomplish anything; nothing was impossible.

By 1948, only three years after arriving in the United States, Wang had earned a Ph.D. in Physics from Harvard University. After he got his Ph.D., he stayed at Harvard and worked in the Computation Laboratory. It was at this time that he invented the magnetic core. This device was a basic part of computer memory until the use of microchips in the late 1960s.

In 1951 Wang decided that he had had enough of

The Wang Center for the Performing Arts in Boston was named in recognition of An Wang's many contributions. Wang Laboratories' world headquarters (below) is in Lowell, Mass.

working for other people. While he was working at Harvard, he had saved $600. He used this money to start his own company, Wang Laboratories. His first office had a table, chair, and telephone— nothing more.

The business grew steadily. At first Wang sold electronic components. Later he designed and sold calculators the size of typewriters. And he didn't forget what he had learned about hesitating. When it was time to change the company's direction, he acted. When it was time to leave a market, he didn't hesitate. By the late 1960s he had decided that Japanese companies would soon control the calculator market. Wang Laboratories went on to other things, including the personal computer. By 1985, sales for the company had reached $2 billion.

Success didn't change Wang's lifestyle very much. Before he became the owner of a highly successful business, he had lived simply with his wife and three children. Years later, when he was worth more than $1 billion, he still owned only two suits. And he lived in a house that many people thought was too simple for such a successful businessman.

In his autobiography, Wang expressed his belief that "both individuals and corporations have the responsibility to make some positive contribution to the world." Dr. Wang acted on that belief many times by supporting programs for the arts, education, and medical care in the city of Boston. And perhaps more important, he showed that a person could be successful in business without sacrificing personal values.

A Comprehension and Discussion

1. What do you know about Dr. Wang's life before he came to the United States?
2. Why did he start his own business?
3. What kind of businessman was Dr. Wang?
4. How did he live after he became a wealthy man?
5. Why do you think Dr. Wang received a Liberty Medal?

B Vocabulary in Context

Fill in the blanks with the correct word. Make any necessary changes in the form of the word. Use each word only once.

Nouns	Verbs	Adjectives	Adverbs
core	hesitate	entire	steadily
contributions	support	basic	periodically
components	reach		
market			
upheaval			

1. Company sales _____ $1 billion before they started to go down.
2. The _____ class came to the lecture; no one stayed at home.
3. Students take _____ mathematics before they study geometry.
4. The magnetic core was one of his _____ to computer technology.
5. There is no longer a large _____ for typewriters; most people are buying word processors.
6. Sales increased _____; each year they doubled their money.
7. Some people _____ the arts center by working there for free. Others give money.
8. It's important to review _____ what you have already learned.
9. He _____ before making a decision because he didn't understand the problem.
10. The central part of something is the _____.
11. During the _____ in the company, many people lost their jobs.
12. A computer has many _____.

2 Focus on Grammar

The Past Perfect Tense
Had + past participle

Rule	Example
1. Use the past perfect tense to show the relationship between two actions in the past. The past perfect tense indicates the action that took place first.	a. He **had** already **earned** a university degree when he left the country. b. He **had saved** $600 before he quit his job.

(continued)

The Past Perfect Tense (continued)

Rule	Example
2. Adverbs such as *already, finally, just, yet,* and *never* often appear in sentences with the past perfect tense.	a. When he came to the U.S., he **had already learned** to speak English. b. She **had already finished** her studies at the university when she left the country. c. They **had just had** a baby when he decided to start his own business.
3. When the adverbs *before* and *after* are used in a sentence, you may use the past perfect tense, but you do not have to use it. The adverbs tell you which event took place first.	a. **Before** she arrived in New York, she **had worked** in Boston. b. **Before** she arrived in New York, she **worked** in Boston.

A Practice

Complete these sentences, using the past perfect tense.

1. (already/become) When I first met him, he <u>had already become</u> well known.
2. (already/leave) By the time I got to her house, everyone else _____.
3. (be) When he began his studies at the university, he _____ here for just three years.
4. (get) He lost his job because he _____ angry with his boss.
5. (just/return) When I saw her on the street, she _____ from a trip to France.
6. (work) She _____ in the company for just three years when they made her president.
7. (already/got) Three of his brothers _____ their university degrees when he began his studies.
8. (already/write) By the time he was twenty-five, he _____ several books.
9. (fail) They took away his car because he _____ to pay the bills.
10. (not/have) They _____ time to pack before they left.
11. (just/leave) When I arrived, they _____.
12. (visit) By the time he left, he _____ every museum and tourist spot in the city.

B Interact

Work with several of your classmates to act out each of these sentences.

1. She had left by the time I got there.
   She was leaving when I got there.
   She left when I got there.

2. She had already eaten when I got there.
   She was eating when I got there.
   She ate when I got there.
3. She had just stood up when I came into the room.
   She was standing up when I came into the room.
   She stood up when I came into the room.
4. When I arrived, he had just made some coffee.
   When I arrived, he was making coffee.
   When I arrived, he made some coffee.

C Interact

Practice this dialogue with a partner.

A: Guess what? I've just <u>gotten a new job</u>.
B: That's great. But don't get too excited.
A: Why not?
B: Well, I had just <u>gotten a new job</u> last year, and then <u>the company went out of business</u>.

A: Guess what? I've just _____.
B: That's great. But don't get too excited.
A: Why not?
B: Well, I had just _____ last year and then _____.

1. ask Victoria to marry me
2. start a new business
3. find $100
4. put $1000 in the bank
5. finish packing my suitcase to go on vacation
6. get a new car
7. find a new apartment
8. _____

Practice

Make up answers to the following questions, using the past perfect tense.

1. Why didn't you have dinner with your parents last night?
   They had already eaten by the time I got home.
2. Why didn't you help with the housework?

3. Why didn't you get your car from the mechanic?

4. Why didn't you buy that coat?

5. Why didn't they eat out last night?

6. Why didn't he put the money in the bank?

7. Why didn't you go to the movies last night?

8. Why didn't you get anything to eat at the party?

9. She didn't pass the course. Do you know why?

10. They took away their son's bicycle. Why was that?

E **Interact**

Practice this dialogue with a partner.

A: Were you able to help Roger <u>fix the car</u>?
B: Well, I went over but I couldn't help him.
A: Why not? Had he <u>fixed the car</u> already?
B: No, he'd <u>taken it to the junkyard</u>.

A: Were you able to help Roger _____?
B: Well, I went over but I couldn't help him.
A: Why not? Had he _____ already?
B: No, he'd _____.

1. cook dinner
2. sell his furniture
3. put the boat in the water
4. get ready for the party
5. do his homework
6. replace the window
7. start the car
8. find his suit
9. _____

Use either the past tense or the past perfect tense in the following sentences. In some cases either tense may be possible.

1. When he came to the United States, he (not/have) _did not have_ a job.
2. He (start) _____ his business when he (save) _____ up enough money.
3. By the time he arrived here, the war (end) _____.
4. He (be) _____ a physics student before he (enter) _____ the computer science program.
5. He (get) _____ his Ph.D. by the time he was twenty-three.
6. During his lifetime, he (contribute) _____ money to cultural programs in Boston.
7. Dr. Wang (invent) _____ the magnetic core while he was working at Harvard.
8. It wasn't hard for him to market his invention because he (know) _____ many people in the computer industry.
9. After he became rich, he (not/change) _____ his lifestyle.
10. Dr. Wang (receive) _____ the Liberty Medal in 1986.

G Practice

Read the following paragraph. Then look at the list of events. Number the sentences in each set to show which event took place first.

I had just gotten home from work when I noticed that the lights in my neighbor's living room were on. I decided to go and see if everything was OK because I remembered that my neighbors had left to go on vacation that morning. (They had given me their keys so I could water their plants.) I had just put the key in the lock when I heard a noise behind me. As I was turning around to look, someone hit me over the head. When I woke up, whoever had hit me was gone, and so was my wallet.

a. _____ I saw lights in my neighbor's house.
_____ I got home from work.
b. _____ I went to see if everything was OK.
_____ My neighbors left to go on vacation.
c. _____ I heard a noise behind me.
_____ I put the key in the lock.
_____ Someone hit me.
d. _____ I woke up.
_____ The person left.
_____ The person stole my wallet.

Now, without looking in the book, retell the story to another student. Use your own words.

H **Practice**

Join each pair of sentences, using "by the time" and the past perfect.

Example: His family ate breakfast at 7:00. He came into the kitchen at 7:30.
By the time he came into the kitchen, his family had already eaten.

1. His bus left at 7:45. He arrived at the bus station at 7:50.

2. An important meeting began at 9:00. He got to the meeting at 9:15.

3. His wife went out at 10:45. He phoned her at 11:00.

4. We got to the train station at 9. The train left at 8:30.

5. His boss's plane took off at 4:15. He arrived at the airport with some important papers for his boss at 4:20.

6. The lecture lasted from 1 to 2. He got there at 2:15.

7. They got to the restaurant at 9:45. The restaurant stopped serving at 9:30.

8. It started to rain at 11. He left at 11:15.

3 Focus on Grammar

The Past Perfect Continuous Tense
had + been + verb - ing

Rule	Example
1. Use the past perfect continuous tense to emphasize the duration of an event that took place before another event in the past.	a. We **had been driving** for several hours when the car broke down. b. He **had been complaining** about his job for months before he finally quit.
2. To form the past perfect continuous tense, use *had (not)* + *been* + a present participle.	a. She went to the doctor because she **had been having** trouble sleeping. b. She got the letters back because she **had been sending** them to the wrong address.

A Practice

Use either the past continuous or the past perfect continuous tense in these sentences.

1. They (work) __had been working__ in London for several years before they had to leave the country.
2. They didn't see him on TV because they (watch) _____ the wrong channel.
3. He (feel) _____ sick for a long time before he went to the doctor.
4. He lost his job even though he (not/do) _____ anything wrong.
5. It wasn't taking very long to do the work because everyone (help) _____.
6. Because he (work) _____ at the movie theater, he got to see a lot of free movies.
7. She (study) _____ computer languages while she was working at Wang Laboratories.
8. The satellite (orbit) _____ in space for several years before they were able to fix it.
9. Some of the dancers (dance) _____ for days before they finally stopped the marathon.
10. As soon as she (feel) _____ better, she went back to work.
11. She stayed in bed all day because she (feel) _____ sick.
12. He was exhausted by nine because he (work) _____ outdoors all day.

I See You Never

by Ray Bradbury

In the short story "I See You Never," Ray Bradbury tells of a man who moves from Mexico City to Los Angeles. The man, Mr. Ramirez, lives for several years in the city, staying in the boarding house of a woman named Mrs. O'Brian. In this excerpt from the story, the police have just come to the boarding house to get Mr. Ramirez.

"What happened, Mr. Ramirez?" asked Mrs. O'Brian.

Behind Mrs. O'Brian, as he lifted his eyes, Mr. Ramirez saw the long table laid with clean white linen and set with a platter, cool shining glasses, a water pitcher with ice cubes floating inside it, a bowl of fresh potato salad and one of bananas and oranges, cubed and sugared. At this table sat Mrs. O'Brian's children— her three grown sons, eating and conversing, and her two younger daughters, who were staring at the policemen as they ate.

"I have been here thirty months," said Mr. Ramirez quietly, looking at Mrs. O'Brian's plump hands.

"That's six months too long," said one policeman. "He only had a temporary visa. We've just got around to looking for him."

Soon after Mr. Ramirez had arrived he bought a radio for his little room; evenings, he turned it up very loud and enjoyed it. And he bought a wrist watch and enjoyed that too. And on many nights he had walked silent streets and seen the bright clothes in the windows and bought some of them, and he had seen the jewels and bought some of them for his few lady friends. And he had gone to picture shows five nights a week for a while. Then, also, he had ridden the street-cars— all night some nights— smelling the electricity, his dark eyes moving over the advertisements, feeling the wheels rumble under him, watching the little sleeping houses and big hotels slip by. Besides that, he had gone to large restaurants, where he had eaten many-course dinners, and to the opera and the theater. And he had bought a car, which later, when he forgot to pay for it, the dealer had driven off angrily from in front of the rooming house.

"So here I am," said Mr. Ramirez now, "to tell you I must give up my

room, Mrs. O'Brian. I come to get my baggage and clothes and go with these men."

"Back to Mexico?"

"Yes. To Lagos. That is a little town north of Mexico City."

"I'm sorry, Mr. Ramirez."

"I'm packed," said Mr. Ramirez hoarsely, blinking his dark eyes rapidly and moving his hands helplessly before him. The policemen did not touch him. There was no necessity for that.

"Here is the key, Mrs. O'Brian," Mr. Ramirez said. "I have my bag already."

Mrs. O'Brian, for the first time, noticed a suitcase standing behind him on the porch.

Mr. Ramirez looked in again at the huge kitchen, at the bright silver cutlery and the young people eating and the shining waxed floor. He turned and looked for a long moment at the apartment house next door, rising up three stories, high and beautiful. He looked at the balconies and fire escapes and back-porch stairs, at the lines of laundry snapping in the wind.

"You've been a good tenant," said Mrs. O'Brian.

"Thank you, thank you, Mrs. O'Brian," he said softly.

1. How long had Mr. Ramirez lived at Mrs. O'Brian's rooming house?
2. What kinds of things had he done for entertainment?
3. Why did the policemen come to Mrs. O'Brian's house?
4. Why did Mr. Ramirez have to leave?

Decide if these sentences are true or false.

5. Mr. Ramirez had to leave the country because he had done
   something wrong.   T   F
6. Mr. Ramirez had been in the United States for less than
   two years.   T   F
7. The dealer took back Mr. Ramirez's car because he had
   forgotten to pay for it.   T   F
8. The policemen were rough with Mr. Ramirez.   T   F
9. Mr. Ramirez had not been a good tenant.   T   F

B Vocabulary in Context

Choose the word or definition that is closest in meaning to the _italicized_ word.

1. The young girls _stared_ at the policemen.
   a. ask questions   **b.** laugh   **c.** look at for a long time
        about
2. It was only a _temporary_ job, but she could find another job later.
   a. part time   **b.** for a short time **c.** permanent
3. People were _conversing_ in different parts of the room.
   a. talking   **b.** sleeping   **c.** standing
4. He _turned up_ the radio so that he could hear the music.
   a. decreased the   **b.** increased the   **c.** shut off
        volume   volume
5. He had to _give up_ his car because he couldn't pay for it.
   a. destroy   **b.** use   **c.** return
6. He was _hoarse_ after singing all evening.
   a. soft   **b.** rough sounding   **c.** loud
7. The car _dealer_ showed him several used cars.
   a. owner   **b.** salesperson   **c.** mechanic
8. The _tenants_ must pay at the beginning of the month.
   a. owners   **b.** people who   **c.** people who pay rent
                                    are rich

5 Listening 📼

Listen to "Goodbye Again," a folk song by John Denver. Then listen to information about the life of this popular musician, and choose the answer that best completes these sentences.

1. John Denver is
   a. a famous architect.
   b. a well-known American folk singer.
   c. the owner of a restaurant in California.
2. John Denver was born in 1943 in
   a. Denver, Colorado.
   b. Los Angeles, California.
   c. Roswell, New Mexico.
3. John wanted to be a singer
   a. from the time he was a college student.
   b. since 1943.
   c. from the time he started working.
4. When John left college he had two jobs. They were
   a. being a draftsman and a singer.
   b. being an architect and working for RCA.
   c. working for an air line and singing in coffee houses.
5. Before John had a career singing alone he
   a. sang with his wife.
   b. sang with the Chad Mitchell Trio.
   c. played guitar for other famous singers.
6. John's song "Goodbye Again" tells about
   a. his love for Colorado.
   b. leaving college.
   c. his travels and feelings about being away from home.

Now listen to these short dialogues. Each one is a conversation between two people who are saying goodbye to each other. Decide if you think the two people are saying goodbye for a long time or for a short time.

1. long time   short time
2. long time   short time
3. long time   short time
4. long time   short time
5. long time   short time

6 Pronunciation

Jazz Chant

I Hate To Say Goodbye

Would you excuse me please? I really have to run.

Would you excuse me please? I really have to run.

Would you excuse me please? I really have to run.

No, no. Please don't run. You've really just come.

It's been very nice talking to you, but I really must rush off.

It's been very nice talking to you, but I really must rush off.

It's been very nice talking to you, but I really must rush off.

No, no. Don't rush off. I really want to talk.

I hope you don't mind, but I really should go.

I hope you don't mind, but I really should go.

I hope you don't mind, but I really should go.

No, no. Please don't go. There's really so much more to know.

7 Writing

Choose a situation in which two people might have to say goodbye to each other. Then decide what each person would say. Write your dialogue and ask two students to perform it for the rest of the class. Have the class guess what the situation is.

8 Get Together

With your classmates, make a list of problems that a child might have moving to a new country. Then, make a list of the problems an adult might have moving to a new country. Are the problems the same for children and adults? Which problems do you think would be the most difficult to overcome?

UNIT 7 VOCABULARY

Nouns
autobiography
belief
component
computer
contribution
core
corporation
dealer
device
direction
market
owner
responsibility
success

tenant
upheaval
value

Verbs
accomplish
control
converse
earn
experience
express
hesitate
reach
sacrifice

stare
support
survive
own

Adjectives
basic
entire
hoarse
nervous
personal
positive
successful
temporary

Adverbs
awhile
highly
immediately
periodically
simply
steadily

Phrasal verbs
give up
go on (to)
turn up

COMMUNICATION
Describing/identifying people by location/present action • Expressing, justifying opinions • Asking questions as a stimulus in a conversation • Discussing observed differences between items

GRAMMAR
Identifying vs. non-identifying relative clauses • Relative pronouns as subjects of verbs • Relative pronouns as objects

What's in a Name?

Place names in the United States came from a variety of sources. Can you find examples of these names on the map?

- a town with a name of something that you could eat
- a town that doesn't sound like a pleasant place in which to live

- a town that sounds like a nice place in which to live
- a town that has a name of something you could wear

- a good place to visit if you can't swim

Answers: Pie Town, Noodle, Two Egg; Burnt Ranch, Hell, Cut and Shoot; Green Grass, Sweet Home; Mexican Hat; Shallow water.

The Story Behind the Name

James Madison

Marquis de Lafayette

At first only a few people lived near the lake. Then more people arrived and built houses, and soon there was a small town. No one, however, had given the town a name. The people who lived in the area had plenty of suggestions, but they could never agree on any one name. Soon a real dispute, or argument, arose about the town's name. Because everyone was arguing so much, someone finally suggested the name "Disputanta," from the word *dispute*. Everyone liked the name and so the town became Disputanta, Tennessee. Not all place names in the United States had such unusual beginnings, but there are some interesting stories behind many of the names.

People's names

Many places in the United States got their names from people who were important or who did something special. The first British settlers gave names to many places along the east coast of the United States, and they often chose names that honored the aristocracy back in England. New York, for example, honors the Duke of York, who was the son of King Charles I.

After the Revolutionary War, the citizens of the new United States weren't so eager to honor the English anymore. Instead, they began choosing names that honored national heroes. There are now twenty-seven towns or cities called Madison in honor of James Madison, who was the fourth President of the United States. Twenty-six places took the name Washington in honor of the first U.S. President.

French settlers who came to the United States honored people like Lafayette, the French general who fought in the Revolutionary War. In fact, so

A road sign in Lynchville, Maine

many towns chose the name Lafayette that the post office finally said, "No more Lafayettes." But this didn't stop people from honoring Lafayette. They just made a few minor changes in the name. Thus, we have places like Lafayette Hill, Fayette, and Fayette Springs.

Many other place names in the United States came from Spanish explorers and settlers. The Spanish often chose names that honored religious figures. Look at a map of the western United States and you'll find many names like San Jose, Santa Barbara, and San Franciso.

Indian names

Many place names in the United States came from the Indians who lived in the area. Twenty-six of the fifty states have names that came from Indian words. Massachusetts, for example, comes from an Algonquian Indian word that means "great mountain place." Texas comes from an Indian word that means "friends."

Names of faraway places

Many towns in the United States have the same names as cities in other countries. If you drive around the state of Maine, for example, you can travel from Paris through Belgrade to Vienna and Rome. And this will only take a few hours. Drive for another hour and you can go to China. But some of these names don't actually refer to places faraway. Paris, Maine, for example, took its name from Alfron Paris, a politician who helped Maine to become a state. And Poland, Maine took its name from a local Indian chief by the name of Polan, not from the country in Europe.

Descriptive names

Some people looked at the animals, plants, and landscape when they were trying to think of a name. This is why you find places with names like Cranberry Lake, Bird Rock, and Buffalo. Other places had names that were supposed to attract settlers. That's why you find names like Richlands, Good Hope, and Sweetwater. Doesn't this make you wonder how places like Death Valley, Boring, and Peculiar got their names?

A | Comprehension and Discussion

1. How did the town of Disputanta get its name?
2. Many of the early settlers did not choose Indian names for their towns and rivers. Why do you think this was so?
3. When did people stop giving British names to places? Why?
4. According to the reading, why did people name their town Richlands?
5. How did the town or city that you live in get its name?

B | Vocabulary in Context

Choose the word or definition that is closest in meaning to the *italicized* word.

1. After the war, people weren't *eager* to name states after English kings.
   a. tired of   **b.** interested in   **c.** able
2. The *dispute* about the town's name lasted for months.
   a. disagreement   **b.** decision   **c.** talk
3. The name of the state of New York *honors* the Duke of York.
   a. makes fun of   **b.** shows respect for   **c.** is the same as
4. The *citizens* of the United States chose place names that honored national heroes.
   a. visitors   **b.** important people   **c.** legal residents
5. They began choosing names that honored national *heroes*.
   a. people who are remembered for doing something brave or good   **b.** the first people to come to a country   **c.** people who make the laws for a country
6. The people who *explored* the new land had to name many places.
   a. visited   **b.** lived in   **c.** first studied
7. In the early years, the British *settlers* stayed along the east coast of the United States.
   a. visitors   **b.** first people to live in an area   **c.** heroes
8. Poland, Maine got its name from a *local* Indian chief.
   a. from the area   **b.** famous   **c.** popular

C Vocabulary in Context

Fill in the blanks with the correct word. Use each word only once. Make any necessary changes in the form of the word.

Nouns	Verbs	Adjectives
settlers	honor	local
dispute	explore	eager
citizen		
hero		

1. He is _____ to visit New York City and see the Statue of Liberty and the Empire State Building.
2. One way to _____ a person is to do something special for him or her.
3. A _____ telephone call costs less than a long-distance call.
4. They have been involved in a _____ for many years. They both think they own the same piece of land.
5. If you are a _____ of the United States, you must pay taxes.
6. Before the _____ arrived from England, Indians had been living in the area.
7. Many people _____ North America looking for a route to the Far East.
8. She was a _____ to many people because she worked to save many sick children.

2 Focus on Grammar

Identifying vs. Non-identifying Relative Clauses

Rule	Example
1. A relative clause gives more information about a noun or pronoun in the sentence.	a. South Carolina's name honors Charles I, **who was the King of England.** b. I need the map **that is on the table**.

(continued)

Identifying vs. Non-identifying Relative Clauses (continued)

Rule	Example
2. There are two kinds of relative clauses. An *identifying* relative clause gives necessary information. The sentence will not make sense if the identifying clause is removed. A *non-identifying* relative clause gives extra information. A non-identifying clause can be omitted without changing the meaning of the sentence.	*identifying clause* a. Everyone **who lives in the town** came from Sweden. b. Can you think of a town **that has a Spanish name**? *non-identifying clause* c. Massachusetts, **which is in New England**, has an Indian name.
3. Identifying clauses are never set off with commas (a). Non-identifying clauses are always set off with commas (b).	a. People **who are under sixteen** cannot drive cars, in most states. b. My brother, **who is fifteen**, cannot drive.

A | Practice

Copy these sentences. Underline the relative clause in each sentence. Then draw an arrow to the word it describes.

> *Example:* Many places in the United States took their names from people <u>who were famous leaders.</u>

1. The state of Alabama got its name from an Indian tribe that lived in the area.

2. The people who named California got the name from a Spanish poem, *Las Sergas de Esplandián,* by Garcia Ordónez de Montalvo.

3. Colorado got its name from a Spanish word that means "the color red."

4. The name of the state of Connecticut comes from the Indian word "Quinnehtukqut," which means "beside the long river."

5. Georgia was named after George II, who was King of England.

6. The state of Louisiana honors Louis XIV, who was King of France.

7. Henrietta Maria, who was queen of Charles I of England, gave her name to the state of Maryland.

8. Montana is another state that got its name from the Spanish language.

9. Ohio is an Indian word that means "great river."

10. The state of Vermont got its name from the French words "vert mont," which mean "green mountain."

Mountains in Vermont

B Practice

Find the relative clause in each of the sentences below. Decide if the clause is an identifying clause or a non-identifying clause. If it is an identifying clause, add commas to the sentence.

1. People who have been drinking should not drive.
2. The town that I live in has a population of 30,000.
3. Her husband who is from Laos is an engineer.
4. Their only daughter who is sixteen has a driver's license now.
5. They bought a bicycle for their daughter who is at the university.
6. The plant that has yellow flowers is called "celandine."
7. The book that he wrote is in the library.
8. I got help from my sister who is a lawyer.
9. The town is named after Madison who was the fourth President of the U.S.
10. I don't know anyone who likes anchovies.

C Practice

Go back to the reading at the beginning of the unit. Find and copy the relative clauses. Count the number of identifying clauses. How many did you find?

3 Focus on Grammar

Relative Pronouns as Subjects of Verbs
who, which, that

Rule	Example
1. Relative clauses allow you to combine two simple sentences into one long sentence. The relative pronoun *who, which,* or *that* can replace the subject in one of the original simple sentences.	a. Kentucky gets its name from an Indian word. **The Indian word** means "meadowland." Kentucky gets its name from an Indian word **that** means "meadowland." b. They named the town after Alfron Paris. **Alfron Paris** was a politician in Maine. They named the town after Alfron Paris, **who** was a politician in Maine.
2. In an identifying clause, use *who* or sometimes *that* to refer to a person. Use *that* to refer to an animal or thing. In a non-identifying clause, use *who* to refer to a person. Use *which* to refer to an animal or thing. *That* is never used to introduce a non-identifying clause.	a. Alfron Paris was the politician **who (that)** helped Maine to become a state. b. Cranberry Lake got its name from a fruit **that** grows in the area. c. The President, **who** is very popular, might get elected again. d. My car, **which** is now ten years old, still runs perfectly.

A Practice

Combine each pair of sentences, using *that, which,* or *who,* to write a new sentence. Use commas in your new sentence if you are using a non-identifying clause.

1. In 1942, an Oklahoma town named itself after Gene Autry. Gene Autry was a popular actor in western movies.
   In 1942, an Oklahoma town named itself after Gene Autry, who was a popular actor in Western movies.

2. Jim Thorpe was one of America's greatest athletes. One Pennsylvania town named itself after Jim Thorpe.

3. One area in California is famous for experimentation with computers and silicon chips. This area is called Silicon Valley.

4. TV Mountain in Montana got its name from a TV transmitter. The TV transmitter stands on a nearby mountain.

5. Tin Mountain, California, celebrates the mining industry. The industry was important in the 19th century.

6. Pabst Mountain got its name from two mountain climbers. The climbers drank a bottle of Pabst Beer when they got to the top of the mountain.

7. The city of Carlsbad, New Mexico, has the nickname the cavern city. Carlsbad, New Mexico, has many limestone caves.

8. San Francisco is known as the Bay City. It surrounds a large natural harbor.

B Practice

Complete these sentences by adding an identifying clause. Use *who* or *that* to introduce the clause.

1. I live in a town _____*that is near a lake*_____.
2. I have a good friend _____.
3. I know someone in the class _____.
4. I like people _____.
5. I would like to have a car _____.
6. I enjoy movies _____.
7. I don't like food _____.
8. I don't get along with people _____.
9. I would like to go to a place _____.
10. I have never known a person _____.

C Interact

Practice these dialogues with a partner.

A: I really didn't like the <u>movie</u> that I <u>saw</u> last night.
B: Really? Why not?
A: Oh, I don't know. I guess <u>it was just too violent</u>.

A: I really didn't like the _____ that I _____ last night.
B: Really? Why not?
A: Oh, I don't know. I guess _____.

1. book	5. restaurant
2. TV show	6. concert
3. party	7. people
4. food	8. _____

Use the information in the chart to ask and answer questions about each of these state names. Use *that* in your sentences.

> *Example:* What does the name "Mississippi" mean?
> "Mississippi" is an Indian word that means "big river."

What does the name _____ mean?
_____ is an _____ word that means _____.

State Name	Type of Word	Meaning
Mississippi	Indian (Algonquian)	big river
Alaska	Aleut	sea-breaker
Colorado	Spanish	red color
Texas	Indian	friends or allies
Florida	Spanish	feast of flowers
Nevada	Spanish	snow-capped
Pennsylvania	English	Penn's woods
Vermont	French	green mountain
Nebraska	Indian (Oto)	flat water
Montana	Spanish	mountainous

Now ask and answer questions about the names of these cities.

Name	Type of Word	Meaning
San Salvador (El Salvador)	Spanish	Holy Savior
Addis Ababa (Ethiopia)	Amharic	new flower
Libreville (Gabon)	French	free town
Godthaab (Greenland)	Scandinavian	good hope
Jakarta (Indonesia)	Sanskrit	place of victory
Dublin (Ireland)	Gaelic	black pool
Tokyo (Japan)	Japanese	eastern capital
Phnom Penh (Kampuchea)	Khmer	mountain of abundance
Nairobi (Kenya)	Swahili	swamp
Beirut (Lebanon)	Greek	well or spring

E | Interact

Practice this dialogue with a partner. Imagine that you are in the room with the people in the picture.

A: Have you met <u>my friend John yet</u>?
B: No, I haven't. Which one is <u>he</u>?
A: <u>He's</u> the one who <u>is standing by the table and drinking a coke</u>.

A: Have you met _____?
B: No, I haven't. Which one is _____?
A: _____ the one who _____.

4 Focus on Grammar

Relative Pronouns as Objects
who(m), which, that

Rule	Example
1. Use the relative pronoun *who(m)*, *which*, or *that* as the object of a verb. Use *who(m)* or *that* to refer to people. Use *that* or *which* to refer to things.	a. The Spanish named places for saints **whom (that)** they wanted to honor. b. The car **that** I bought is small. c. This suit, **which** I just bought, is 100% wool.
2. Use the relative pronoun *whom* or *which* as the object of a preposition. Use *whom* to refer to people. Use *which* to refer to things.	a. The man **after whom** they named the town was a famous politician. b. The movie **in which** he has a role will be released soon.
3. In an identifying clause, a relative pronoun that is the object of a verb may sometimes be omitted. This is common in speaking. A relative pronoun that is the object of a preposition may also be omitted. The preposition then goes at the end of the clause.	a. The town (that) they visited had a strange name. b. The people (whom) I am staying with speak Portuguese. c. The street on which she lives has several stores. The street she lives on has several stores.

A Practice

Combine each pair of sentences to make a new sentence.

> *Example:* The man speaks Chinese. You just met him.
> *The man whom you just met speaks Chinese.*

1. The state has an Indian name. They live in the state.

2. The name honors the Duke of York. The early British settlers chose the name.

3. The woman is called Maria. I am sitting next to her.

4. The company makes cars. I work for the company.

5. The man is from Chile. My sister is married to him.

6. He knows the people. I work with the people now.

7. I attended the school. My father graduated from the school.

8. They found the wallet. She lost the wallet last week.

9. I voted for the man. You voted for the man.

10. I broke the glass vase. My sister gave it to me for my birthday.

B Practice

Complete these sentences. Pay careful attention to the use of *who* and *whom*.

> *Example:* The settlers whom you read about came here in the 1800's.
> The settlers who came here in the 1800's named many places.

1. The singer whom _____.
2. The singer who _____.
3. The author whom _____.
4. The author who _____.
5. Napoleon was a leader who _____.
6. Napoleon was a leader whom _____.
7. I am looking for someone who _____.
8. I am looking for someone whom _____.

C Get Together

Work with a partner. Tell your partner to look at the picture on page 145 while you look at the picture on page 143. You should not look at each other's picture.

Your picture is almost the same as your partner's picture, but there are five minor differences. Try to find the differences. Use sentences with *who*, *that*, and *which*.

> *Example:* In your picture, does the man who is writing have a beard?

5 Remember

Verb Tenses

Fill in the blanks with the correct form of the verb in parentheses.

1. In 1917 Thomas W. Bicknell, a wealthy New Yorker, offered to give a library to any town that (name) _____*named*_____ itself "Bicknell." Thurber, Utah (be) _____ willing to change its name in order to get a new library but so was Grayson, Utah. Mr. Bicknell (not/want) _____ two towns in Utah with his name, but he had an interesting solution. The town of Thurber (become) _____ "Bicknell" and the town of Grayson (take) _____ Mrs. Bicknell's maiden name, which was "Blanding." The two towns then divided the library books.

2. There (be) _____ still a town in Massachusetts called Canton. When the first settlers of this town (look) _____ for a name, one person insisted on the name Canton. He not/be _____ from Canton, China; he (never/be) _____ there. But he had decided that if you dug a hole in the town center, you (come out) _____ in Canton, China.

(continued on p. 143)

3. In the late 1700s a group of Englishmen were exploring the coast of Alaska. Each day groups of men (go) _____ ashore and made notes and drawings of the land. When they (come) _____ back to the ship in the afternoon, they gave their notes and drawings to mapmakers who put the information together on large maps. One day, one of the men was exploring an area that (not/have) _____ a name. To remind the mapmaker of this, he (write) _____ "Name" on the map. But he (not/write) _____ it very neatly. When the mapmaker (draw) _____ the large map, he wrote "Nome" in the area. The area (be) _____ still called Nome today.

4. In 1510 Garcia Ordónez de Montalvo (write) _____ a novel called *Las Sergas de Esplandián*. The story (describe) _____ a mythical island called "California." In the 1560s the Spanish explorer Hernandez Cortés (travel) _____ along the western coast of the Americas. When he (arrive) _____ at the southern end of California, he thought it looked like the mythical island in the book and so he (name) _____ it California. Later explorers discovered that this (be) _____ not an island, but the name stayed and today it (be) _____ the state of California.

6 Writing

Get together with another student. Write your own story which explains how the towns "Boring" and "Peculiar" got their names. Share your story with your classmates.

7 Pronunciation

/w/ /y/ /h/

Repeat these words.

1. we	4. one	7. between
2. wonder	5. question	8. someone
3. welcome	6. equal	9. language

Now repeat these words.

1. yes	3. university	5. you
2. young	4. review	6. few

Now repeat these words.

1. here	3. who	5. unhappy
2. house	4. ahead	6. behind

Repeat these contrasting words.

1. wet   yet
2. wore   yore
3. Wes   yes
4. air   hair
5. all   hall
6. ill   hill
7. ear   hear

Now repeat these sentences.

1. Why do you wear that sweater?
2. Why do you always wear that yellow wool sweater?
3. He used to work here.
4. He used to work here, but he went away yesterday.

Talk with your partner. How is this picture different from the picture your partner is looking at?

What's Your Name?

In the 1980s the ten most popular names for baby boys in the United States were Michael, Matthew, Christopher, Brian, David, Adam, Andrew, Daniel, Jason, and Joshua. For girls, the most popular names were Jennifer, Sarah, Jessica, Amanda, Nicole, Ashley, Megan, Melissa, Katherine, and Stephanie.

Would you give a child a popular name or would you choose a name that is a little different? Some psychologists believe that the name you get influences your personality and even your career choice. According to these psychologists, children who have familiar names like Michael and Christopher are associated with strength and competence. On the other hand, unusual names like Reginald and Horace remind people of weakness and ineptitude.

Another study, however, showed that a large proportion of U.S. business leaders had unusual first names. Once in awhile a Bob, Joe, or John gets to the top of a company. But in a study of 1000 companies, many of the top executives had less familiar names. Dwayne, Barry, Craig, and Dorsey are a few of the names you might see on a list of top executives. And it is not uncommon to see an initial instead of a first name. Think of the highly successful businessmen J. Paul Getty and H.H. Wetzel. Why did they use initials instead of their full names?

The importance of names is clear if you think about people who are in entertainment. Why have so many changed their names? Did they really think they couldn't become famous with their original names? Many entertainers changed their names to make

them more unusual. Think of people like Zsa Zsa Gabor, Meryl Streep, and Sissy Spacek. Zsa Zsa Gabor started out life with a less exotic name— Sari Gabor. Meryl Streep and Sissy Spacek made their real names— Mary Louise Streep and Mary Elizabeth Spacek— just a little more unusual. You may not have heard of Allen Stewart Konigsberg, Sofia Scicolone, or Leslie Townes Hope. But you have probably seen them in the movies as Woody Allen, Sophia Loren, and Bob Hope.

Perhaps the whole name-giving process should change. In one culture in the past, every time a person had an important experience, he added a new name to his identity. An elderly person who had lived a rich life might therefore have nine or ten names. In one Indian tribe, names changed with the coming of each winter and summer. Maybe these aren't such bad ideas. Maybe we should all have the chance to change our names once in a while.

A Comprehension and Discussion

1. Do you think that a person's name affects his personality? Why or why not?
2. Do you know why your parents chose your name?
3. Do you know anyone who has changed his or her name? Why do people sometimes change their names?

B Vocabulary in Context

Choose the word that is closest in meaning to the *italicized* word.

1. She knows a lot about business. Her opinions will *influence* my decision.
   a. control   **b.** give strength to   **c.** have an effect on
2. He is a *competent* sailor. He'll probably never win any races, but he will always get home safely.
   a. lazy   **b.** superb   **c.** skilled
3. His *ineptitude* in mathematics caused him to lose his job.
   a. lack of ability **b.** laziness   **c.** success

4. The *proportion* of the people in the class who own cars is high.
   a. share   b. ability   c. section
5. He is a *highly* successful businessperson.
   a. strangely   b. very   c. unfairly
6. Because her *original* name was difficult to pronounce, she changed it.
   a. last   b. new   c. first
7. *Exotic* names are difficult to forget.
   a. simple   b. strange   c. long
8. He has had a very *rich* life.
   a. expensive   b. satisfactory   c. interesting

9 Listening

You are going to hear a conversation between two students, Michael and Juan. Juan is a new student at the school; his new friend Michael is showing him around. As you listen to the dialogue, make notes about each person who is mentioned. When you have heard the dialogue twice, answer the questions below.

1. The person who is sitting behind Gloria is _____.
   a. Bob
   b. Juan
   c. Fernando
2. If you want some information about music, you should ask _____.
   a. Bob
   b. the girl who is reading the letter
   c. the girl who is sitting with Fernando
3. Bob is going to sit with the girl _____.
   a. who is reading a letter
   b. who is from Puerto Rico
   c. who is called Sonia
4. If you have a question about your homework, you should probably ask _____.
   a. the boy who is sitting with Gloria
   b. Sonia
   c. the boy who is sitting with Sonia
5. The boy who knows a lot about music is _____.
   a. sitting with Sonia
   b. Fernando
   c. Danny
6. Juan and Michael are going to talk with _____.
   a. the musician who is in the back of the cafeteria
   b. the girl who is reading a letter
   c. the boy who is waving his hand

10 | Get Together

Divide into small groups. Use the map below to make 10 identification questions about U.S. geography. Then, exchange questions with another group. See how fast you can answer their questions.

> *Examples:* What is the river that goes between Tennessee and Arkansas?
> What is the state that extends farthest to the east?
> What is the name of a state that begins with C?
> What is the name of a state that is on the border of Canada?

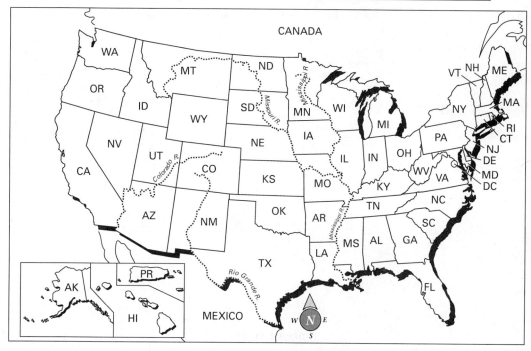

State Name Abbreviations

State	Abbr.	State	Abbr.	State	Abbr.	State	Abbr.
Alabama	AL	Indiana	IN	Nebraska	NE	South Carolina	SC
Alaska	AK	Iowa	IA	Nevada	NV	South Dakota	SD
Arizona	AZ	Kansas	KS	New Hampshire	NH	Tennessee	TN
Arkansas	AR	Kentucky	KY	New Jersey	NJ	Texas	TX
California	CA	Louisiana	LA	New Mexico	NM	Utah	UT
Colorado	CO	Maine	ME	New York	NY	Vermont	VT
Connecticut	CT	Maryland	MD	North Carolina	NC	Virginia	VA
Delaware	DE	Massachusetts	MA	North Dakota	ND	Washington	WA
Florida	FL	Michigan	MI	Ohio	OH	West Virginia	WV
Georgia	GA	Minnesota	MN	Oklahoma	OK	Wisconsin	WI
Hawaii	HI	Mississippi	MS	Oregon	OR	Wyoming	WY
Idaho	ID	Missouri	MO	Pennsylvania	PA	District of Columbia	DC
Illinois	IL	Montana	MT	Rhode Island	RI	Puerto Rico	PR

UNIT 8 VOCABULARY

Nouns
athlete
career
citizen
chief
competence
executive
explorer
hero
identity
ineptitude
landscape
personality
politician

process
proportion
psychologist
settler
solution
suggestion

Verbs
associate with
attract
argue
dispute
explore
honor

influence
refer to

Adjectives
competent
eager
exotic
familiar
famous
local
loyal
minor
original

popular
rich

Adverbs
actually
faraway
highly

Expressions
On the other hand, . . .
In fact, . . .
Instead, . . .
Thus, . . .

COMMUNICATION
Asking for, granting, denying permission • Encouraging/commanding someone to do something • Offering support

GRAMMAR
Verbs of mandating, permitting, and supporting: *make, have, get, help* • Relative clauses (Review) • Adjective clauses with *whose* • Past tenses (Review) • *Must, have to* (Review)

School Days, New Ways

What do you remember most about your first years in school? What classes did you like best? Did your class ever take any trips outside of the school?

Each of the pictures on this page shows students who are involved in special programs. Can you tell what the students are doing or studying?

PROGRAMS PLUS

Teachers are always trying to come up with new ways to get kids excited about learning. They get students to do special projects, to take trips outside of school, and to participate in many kinds of hands-on activities.

The Egg Program in Hartford, Connecticut

Down the hallway of the school stride four eighth-grade students. Each one is carrying a small basket with a single egg inside. Soon more kids join them— each one of them is also carrying a basket with an egg. The eggs in a basket are part of an innovative school program that is supposed to help young people understand that having a baby is an enormous responsibility.

At the beginning of the program, the instructor puts the students in pairs— one girl and one boy. Each pair gets an egg, which they must take care of for two weeks. For those fourteen days, the students have to take care of the eggs as though they were real babies. Students whose eggs get broken have to start the two weeks all over again with a new egg.

One person in each pair must have the egg with him or her at all times— twenty-four hours a day. At no time can they let the egg be out of sight. "If a teacher catches you without your egg," said one student, "she makes you go get it. They are real strict." The teachers also make the students spend half an hour each day sitting with the egg and just watching it. That can get pretty boring. But it's also something that parents spend a lot of time doing.

Kids say that the program has helped them understand the responsibilities involved in having a child. "It was real hard," said one kid. "You had to think all the time about the egg."

Book It!

It isn't always easy to get children to read. Pizza Hut, however, sponsors a unique program that is helping some sixteen million students in kindergarten through sixth grade to discover the joys of reading. It is called the BOOK IT!® National Reading Incentive Program. The five-month BOOK IT program rewards students with pizza and praise for reaching individual reading goals. In addition, the entire class gets a free pizza party when all students reach their goals in four program months.

Telecommunications

The presence of computers in many schools lets students participate in a unique kind of learning. In one program, students first write introductions about themselves and their school. Then they send this information via computer to students who are living in a different part of the country. Once the students know each other via the computer, teachers have them write and exchange stories about the lifestyle and environment in which they live.

Kids Network

What if you had to help a group of 10-year-olds learn about acid rain? For help, you could turn to National Geographic's Kids Network. Students in the fourth, fifth, and sixth grades do experiments that help them learn about the local environment. Then they send the results via the school computer to a central computer. There the data from different schools are analyzed and sent back to the schools. This lets students compare their findings with the findings from other schools.

Bilingual Schools

In their first years in one bilingual (Spanish and English) program, students study reading, writing, mathematics, social studies, and science in their native language. But these young students also get to practice speaking a second language. Every other day either Spanish or English is the "Language of the Day." During attendance, lining up for lunch and gym, teachers make all of the students in the school use the language of the day. By the third, fourth, and fifth grades, students study in both English and Spanish. One week the teachers have them study in English and the next week in Spanish.

A Comprehension and Discussion

1. What do all of these programs have in common?
2. Do you think the egg program is worthwhile? Why or why not?
3. Which of the programs shows how schools and businesses can work together?
4. Can you think of other ways that businesses could get involved in education?
5. What are some ways that computers are used in education?
6. What do you think are the advantages or disadvantages of a bilingual education?
7. Which of these programs sounds the most interesting? Why?
8. Do you know about any other innovative learning programs? Describe and discuss them.

B Vocabulary in Context

Fill in the blanks with the correct word. Make any necessary changes in the form of the verbs.

Nouns	Verbs	Adjectives
goal	participate	innovative
findings	analyze	enormous
environment		unique
		native
		central

1. Her old car is _____; no one else has a car like it.
2. They often use computers to _____ the data.
3. Pollution from the factories is destroying the _____.
4. Because no one had tried it before, they weren't sure that this _____ program would work.
5. The _____ office of the company is in St. Louis; about 80 percent of the people in the company work in that office.
6. Maria _____ in many school activities last year.

7. The school is _____; there are at least 15,000 students.
8. They took daily temperature readings and made a chart of their _____.
9. From the time he was 16, his _____ has been to become an astronaut.
10. I can write poetry only in my _____ language.

2 Focus on Grammar

Verbs of mandating, permitting, and supporting
Make, let, have, get, and help.
verb + object + verb
verb + object + to + verb

Rule	Example
1. The verbs *make* (meaning to force or to give no choice) and *let* (meaning to allow) are followed by a noun or pronoun and the simple form of the verb.	a. The program is supposed to **make** kids **understand** the responsibilites of parents. b. She **let** him **return** the book he had bought.
2. The verb *have* (meaning to cause someone to do something) is followed by a (pro)noun and the simple form of the verb.	a. Teachers **have** the students **exchange** artwork. b. I think I'll **have** my brother **come** over for dinner.
3. The verb *get* (meaning to cause someone to do something) is followed by a (pro)noun and an infinitive.	a. They **got** him **to do** his homework. b. The program **gets** students **to read** extra books.
4. The verb *help* is followed by a (pro)noun and either the simple form of the verb or an infinitive.	a. She **helped** him **clean** the house. b. She **helped** him **to clean** the house.

A Practice

Complete these sentences, using the correct form of the verb in parentheses.

1. (learn) The program helps kids __*learn* (or *to learn*)__ about geography.
2. (draw) Teachers have students _____ pictures of the environment in which they live.

3. (lift) Could you please help me _____ this box?
4. (come) I don't think I can get him _____ to the party.
5. (use) I don't understand why you won't let me _____ the car.
6. (work) There is nothing I can do to make him _____ harder.
7. (watch) When she was a child, her parents never let her _____ TV.
8. (finish) Is there anything I can do to help you _____ the work faster?
9. (help) I think I'll get my brother _____ me fix the car.
10. (stay) At what age do you think you can let children _____ home alone?
11. (memorize) My ninth grade teacher made me _____ long poems.
12. (come) You should probably get someone _____ and fix the sink.

B Practice

Fill in the blanks with the correct form of the verb in parentheses.

1. The state of Rhode Island has an innovative program to help children (say) ____*say*____ no to drugs. Teachers get students (sign) _____ a pledge, or promise, never to take drugs. In the future, graduates who have never used drugs can win college scholarships.

2. In one city in Texas, school officials let teachers (take) _____ time off to visit students' homes. The teachers try to get the parents of these students (become) _____ more involved in their children's education.

3. Teachers who want to help their students (learn) _____ about other parts of the country can join a national program called CREATE. This five-year-old program has gotten more than 150 schools in 38 states (participate) _____. Teachers have their students (create) _____ pictures of the local environment. Students from different schools then exchange their pictures.

4. Over the years, the Rouge River in Michigan has been badly polluted. One man, however, has been able to get people (take) _____ action to improve the river. In 1986, Jim Murray got a group of businesses, local residents, and government leaders (organize) _____ a huge clean-up of the river. Many volunteers helped (clean) _____ out the trash in the river. In about four hours, they were able to pull out more than 3,000 cubic yards of trash.

Complete these sentences.

1. Dad, please let me _____ *borrow the car* _____.
2. No one can make me _____.
3. I don't think parents should let their children _____.
4. I could help someone _____.
5. When I was a child, my parents wouldn't let me _____.
6. I think it's a good idea to make children _____.
7. I would like to have someone _____.
8. It would be difficult to make someone _____.
9. On weekends, you can never get anyone _____.
10. It is very difficult to get kids _____.

D Interact

Practice this dialogue with a partner.

A: Who are you going to get <u>to fix your car</u>?
B: I don't know. I thought I would let you <u>fix it</u>!
A: Ha! Aren't you nice!

A: Who are you going to get _____?
B: I don't know. I thought I would let you _____!
A: Ha! Aren't you nice!

1. paint your room
2. move your furniture
3. build the bookcase
4. repair the TV
5. take care of your kids
6. pick you up at the airport
7. organize the party
8. _____

E Interact

Fill in four items on each list. Then compare your lists with your classmates' lists. Do you agree or disagree with your classmates' answers?

List 1: Parents should **make** their children . . .

List 2: Parents should **let** their children . . .

List 3: Parents should **help** their children . . .

Everything was broken at the Tanners' house last week. Mr. and Mrs. Tanner aren't very good at fixing things, so they persuaded some of their neighbors to help them.

Look at the pictures and ask and answer questions about the Tanners and their neighbors. Use the word *got,* as in the example.

> *Example:* Who did the Tanners get to fix their kitchen sink?
> They *got* Ellen Parker to fix their kitchen sink.

Ellen Parker

Charles Johnson

Gail Monroe

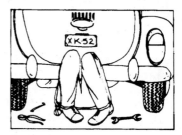
David Turner

Jim Vickers

3 Remember

People **who join the program** must learn to use a computer.

The teacher decides on the number of books **that students will try to read**.

A Practice

Add more information about one of the nouns in each sentence. Copy the sentences and add your information as in the example.

> *that he lost*
> *Example:* The coat ^ cost a lot of money.

1. The program was very interesting.

2. The students were punished.

3. The students got a free pizza party.

4. The pictures showed the environment.

5. Everyone learned more about acid rain.

6. The candidate had done ocean research.

7. The information is confidential.

8. The people have to fill out a form.

9. Some people have trouble making ends meet.

10. The satellite orbited earth.

11. The watch belonged to my grandfather.

12. Men and women learned to sleep while dancing.

For each sentence, choose an appropriate relative clause from the list on the right. Write the letter of the clause. You may use an answer more than once.

1. People _____ cannot become astronauts.
2. People _____ are not supposed to drive.
3. Children _____ have trouble at school.
4. I think people _____ are crazy.
5. People _____ should pay attention to their body rhythms.
6. People _____ will probably live longer.
7. Kids _____ can study in a bilingual program.
8. People _____ can still accomplish a lot.

a. who like fads
b. who have been drinking
c. who are over 40
d. who are taking medicine
e. who watch too much TV
f. who are persistent
g. who don't speak English
h. who don't smoke

4 Focus on Grammar

Adjective Clauses with *Whose*

Rule	Example
Whose is the possessive form of *who*. *Whose* sometimes introduces an adjective clause.	a. I have a friend **whose** degree is in physics. I have a friend. Her degree is in physics. b. Students **whose** grades are high can take an advanced class. (Students can take an advanced course if their grades are high.) c. Students **whose** work is done can leave now.

A Practice

Each of the programs in the left column on the next page will appeal to a certain type of person. Match the programs with the people who are described in the right column. Then make sentences with the information, using *might want to* and an appropriate verb. Some of the programs may appeal to several of the people. Try to find at least one program for each person.

> *Example:* A person whose job is in bilingual education might want to take a one-day seminar on teaching in Spanish and English.

_____ **1.**	a baseball/basketball camp	**a.** a person whose job is in bilingual education
_____ **2.**	a conference on robotics	**b.** someone whose university degree is in oceanography
_____ **3.**	a one-week program on a boat	**c.** children whose interest is in sports
_____ **4.**	a one-day seminar on teaching in Spanish and English	**d.** children whose native language is English
_____ **5.**	a video on health foods	**e.** children whose parents work
_____ **6.**	a contest to get children to read more books	**f.** someone whose background is in engineering
_____ **7.**	an after-school recreation program	**g.** children whose reading ability is low
_____ **8.**	a program on money management	**h.** someone whose eating habits are unhealthy
		i. a person whose budget doesn't work

5 Remember

Past Tenses

Rule Past Tense	Example They **were** in the program for three months. (They are no longer in the program.) He **got** the job in 1989.
Past Continuous Tense	They **were waiting** for me when I arrived. Someone **was singing** outside my window. Did you hear?
Present Perfect Tense	They **have been** in the program for three months. (They are still in the program.) I **have known** him since 1989.
Past Perfect Tense	He lost his job because **he had not** worked very hard. He **had** already **left** by the time I got home.

Use the simple past, present perfect or past perfect tense in the following sentences.

1. The program (be) ___has been___ in existence for five years. This year there are 500 children in the program.
2. Schools first (use) _____ the Kids Network in 1989.
3. The National Geographic Society (spend) _____ many months writing the program before it was used in classrooms.
4. The students (analyze) _____ the data by the time the instructor arrived.
5. After they (meet) _____ their reading goal, they had a party at the restaurant.
6. The students (read) _____ 200 extra books since February.
7. The students got to have a pizza party because they (meet) _____ their reading goal.
8. Many schools (join) _____ the program so far.
9. He got on the bus as soon as it (arrive) _____.
10. None of the students (participate) _____ in the program yet.
11. The students learned about another part of the country while they (use) _____ the computer.
12. He (be) _____ in the program a year ago.

B Practice

Compare the sentences in each pair. For each sentence, explain which action started first.

1. When I got home, my sister was eating dinner.
   When I got home, my sister ate dinner.

2. When I called he was just leaving the house.
   When I called he had just left the house.

3. When he came in, the program had just begun.
   When he came in, the program began.

4. When I woke up, he was leaving.
   When I woke up, he had left.

5. I called him when I heard the news.
   I was calling him when I heard the news.

6. She was doing her homework when class started.
   She had done her homework by the time class started.

6 Remember

Must and Have To

Kids **have to** read a certain number of books within five months.

They **must** write something about the book to show that they have read it.

Students in the program **must not** leave the eggs alone.

The children at that school **don't have to** study a foreign language.

A Practice

Use *must, have to, must not* or *don't/doesn't have to* in these sentences. Some items have more than one correct answer.

1. Children in the "egg program" ____must not____ break the eggs.
2. You _____ be inefficient at work. You might lose your job.
3. In a dance marathon, you _____ stop dancing.
4. You _____ obey the laws of the country in which you live.
5. People _____ answer a census questionnaire, but they should.
6. You _____ take a nap in the afternoon, but it might make you feel more alert.
7. You _____ change your name if you want to become a movie star.
8. We have to make people understand that they _____ drink and drive.
9. You _____ tell anyone about this; it is confidential.
10. To become an astronaut, you _____ have the right qualifications.

7 Writing

Think about your former teachers. What kinds of things did they do to help you to learn? With your classmates, make a list of suggestions for a new teacher. Suggest things that he or she should do with the students.

Now write a description of one of your former teachers. Explain what kinds of things this teacher made you do. How did she or he get you to do your work? In what ways did this teacher help you to learn?

8 Listening

You are going to hear some questions. Listen to each question and choose the most logical answer.

1. **a.** I'm sorry but I need to use it.
   b. I used it before.
2. **a.** I saw her.
   b. I told her that I had an appointment.
3. **a.** Sure.
   b. I didn't let him.
4. **a.** I read it last night.
   b. Sure. Take it.
5. **a.** Because it's cold outside.
   b. Because someone smelled smoke.
6. **a.** I don't know yet.
   b. Yesterday, I think.
7. **a.** No, but I got eight people to do it.
   b. They filled it out.
8. **a.** No, I can't think of anything.
   b. I need help.

9 Pronunciation

/m/ /n/ /ŋ/

Repeat these words.

1. mountain
2. marvelous
3. immediately
4. important
5. swam
6. swimming
7. climb
8. room

Repeat these words.

1. now
2. know
3. knee

4. snowy
5. found
6. thinner

7. Jane
8. expedition
9. ocean

Repeat these words.

1. singing
2. thinking
3. bringing

4. angry
5. hungry
6. tongue

7. wing
8. thing
9. bring

Repeat these contrasting words.

1. me   knee
2. man   Nan
3. mow   know
4. sin   sing
5. win   wing
6. run   rung

Now repeat these sentences.

1. I'm going to climb.
2. I'm going to climb Snowflake Mountain.
3. I'm going to climb Snowflake Mountain with my brother and Jane.

Hardship, Help
for First Time Offenders

(Adapted from an article in *The Christian Science Monitor*, November 10, 1989.)

The following article describes an innovative program for people who have committed nonviolent crimes. The goal of the program is to help these people stay out of trouble in the future.

Seven scared young men stand at attention. They don't dare move. They don't dare look around.

All at once, tough-looking guards begin shouting at them: "Let's go! Move! Get out here! Get going, boy! Line up, boy! Move now, fool!"

The young men— disoriented, confused— rush into a hallway. Guards make them line up, backs to a wall. The young men's frightened eyes glance around the prison, uncertain what will happen next.

This is Day 1 of "shock incarceration," a military-style boot camp for young criminals. Offenders, age 17 to 25, spend 90 days here— instead of five years in state prison. Most are first time offenders. This is their chance to start over fresh: If they do well here, their records are wiped clean. But bad behavior can lead to long-term imprisonment.

The officers who run the program want to help these young men change their lives. Their job is to make the

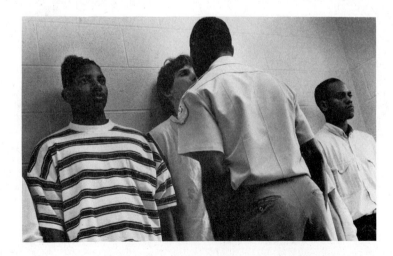

men realize that being in prison is no fun. From the first day, the officers order the men around. They quickly make the men understand who is in charge.

"Let's get one thing straight— now! You'd better understand where you are. From this day forward, the first word out of that mouth is 'sir,' and the last word out of that mouth is 'sir.' Do you understand me?"

The officers quickly let the men know that their behavior in the past was stupid. Under questioning, one prisoner reveals that back home he has a wife and two children.

"Why are you in prison, boy?"

"Sir, taking something, sir."

"Taking what?"

"Motor vehicle, sir."

"What did you do with it, fool?"

"Joy ride, sir."

"How long did you keep it, boy?"

"Sir, four hours, sir."

The answer draws jeers from the prison officers.

"Four hours? You're real smart. You'd better find another line of work, boy. This one's not working out too good. You're setting a real good example for your kids."

The daily routine in this special prison is tough. Prison officers make the men get up at 5 a.m and clean the barracks until they are spotless. Then the men have to do a full day of hard physical labor. When it is time for lunch, the officers let the men break just long enough to eat and then it is back to work. At 4 p.m. the officers make the men do calisthenics for an hour. It's not until 6 that the officers let the men have a free hour— and their only TV of the day. In the evening they get the prisoners to attend educational lectures, but at 10 p.m. lights must be out.

"It's tough. It's real scary," says one young man. "You've got to keep in line. Do what you're told, and when."

Does this kind of military-style, kick-in-the-face training work? Georgia officials say yes. After 90 days here, two out of three prisoners go straight. They get jobs and settle down.

A Comprehension and Discussion

1. Who is this program for?
2. How long will the men stay in this prison?
3. What is life like inside this special prison?
4. What kinds of things do the prison guards make the men do?
5. The officers aren't very nice to the men. Can you find examples of this in the article?
6. What do you think is the toughest or most unpleasant part of the daily prison routine?
7. Reread the dialogue between the officer and the prisoner (7th paragraph). Why is this man in prison?
8. How do you think governments should deal with people who commit non-violent crimes?

B | Vocabulary in Context

Fill in the blanks with the correct word. Change the form of the word if necessary. Use each word once.

Verbs	Adjectives
break	disoriented
reveal	scary
jeer	spotless

1. They _____ for a short lunch.
2. The people _____ at the man because they knew he was lying.
3. When he woke up in a strange house he felt _____.
4. The house was _____ when they finished cleaning it.
5. She couldn't sleep because the movie had been so _____.
6. He asked us not to _____ the good news. He wanted to tell her.

Choose the definition that is closest in meaning to the *italicized* expression.

7. He got a job and *settled down* after his first child was born.
   a. became depressed
   b. lived quietly
   c. moved away
8. There's never any trouble in her classroom. She *keeps* the kids *in line.*
   a. makes them stand in line
   b. ties up the kids
   c. makes them behave
9. "I want you to *get this straight.* You cannot go out until you have finished your work."
   a. be persistent
   b. forget this
   c. understand this
10. After he left prison, he *went straight.*
    a. followed the road
    b. didn't turn
    c. obeyed the law
11. She often reads in the evening to *set an example* for her kids.
    a. provide a model
    b. tell them what to do
    c. yell
12. Everyone stood *at attention* when they raised the flag.
    a. straight and alert
    b. sadly
    c. for a long time

11 New Expressions: Phrasal Verbs

Fill in the blanks with a phrasal verb. Use each verb in the correct form. You may use a verb more than once.

Separable	
order around	*irritate by giving many orders*
start over	*begin again*

Inseparable	
settle down	*become calm*
take care (of)	*care for*

1. It took a while for the children to _____ and go to sleep.
2. While his parents were away, his aunt _____ him.
3. When he was a child, his big brother often _____ him _____.
4. After they sang the song once, they _____ it _____ again.

12 Get Together

Work with two or three of your classmates to design a program for children. Choose one of the program goals below. Then, write a description of your program.

a. To have children learn more about the culture of another country.
b. To help children understand the difficulties of living in a country when you don't understand the language.
c. To discourage young people from starting to smoke.
d. To help children learn how businesses function.
e. To have children learn that plants need sun and water to grow.
f. To have children learn that the level of the ocean at the shore changes regularly during the day (tides).

UNIT 9 VOCABULARY

Nouns
attendance
attention
behavior
chain
computer
environment
experiment
findings
fool
goal
jeer
labor
lifestyle
presence
program
responsibility
result
routine

Verbs
analyze
attend
break
compare
dare
glance
jeer
participate
practice
reveal
rush
succeed

Adjectives
bilingual
boring
central
confused
disoriented
enormous
fresh
innovative
native
real
scary
single
spotless
strict
tough
uncertain
unique

Phrasal Verbs
get up
order around
settle down
shout at
start over
take care (of)

Expressions
get something
  straight
keep in line
go straight
stand at attention
be in charge
be out of sight
set an example

Appendix

A │ Countries, Nationalities, and Languages

Country	Nationality	Language(s)
Algeria	Algerian	Arabic/Berber
Argentina	Argentinian	Spanish
Australia	Australian	English
Bolivia	Bolivian	Spanish
Brazil	Brazilian	Portuguese
Cambodia	Cambodian	Khmer
Canada	Canadian	English/French
Chile	Chilean	Spanish
China	Chinese	Chinese
Colombia	Colombian	Spanish
Costa Rica	Costa Rican	Spanish
Cuba	Cuban	Spanish
Czechoslovakia	Czech	Czech/Slovak
Denmark	Danish	Danish
the Dominican Republic	Dominican	Spanish
Ecuador	Ecuadorean	Spanish
Egypt	Egyptian	Arabic
El Salvador	Salvadorean	Spanish
England	English	English
Ethiopia	Ethiopian	Amharic
France	French	French
Germany	German	German
Great Britain	British	English
Greece	Greek	Greek
Guatemala	Guatemalan	Spanish
Haiti	Haitian	French
Honduras	Honduran	Spanish
India	Indian	Hindi/English
Indonesia	Indonesian	Bahasa Indonesia
Iraq	Iraqi	Arabic
Israel	Israeli	Hebrew/Arabic
Italy	Italian	Italian
Japan	Japanese	Japanese
Jordan	Jordanian	Arabic
Kenya	Kenyan	Swahili
Korea	Korean	Korean
Laos	Laotian	Lao
Lebanon	Lebanese	Arabic
Mexico	Mexican	Spanish
Nicaragua	Nicaraguan	Spanish
Nigeria	Nigerian	English/Hausa/Ibo/Yoruba
Norway	Norwegian	Norwegian
Pakistan	Pakistani	Urdu/Punjabi/English
Panama	Panamanian	Spanish
Paraguay	Paraguayan	Spanish
Peru	Peruvian	Spanish

the Philippines	Filipino	Pilipino/English/Spanish
Poland	Polish	Polish
Portugal	Portuguese	Portuguese
Puerto Rico	Puerto Rican	Spanish
Saudia Arabia	Saudi Arabian	Arabic
the Soviet Union	Soviet/Russian	Russian
Spain	Spanish	Spanish
Sweden	Swedish	Swedish
Syria	Syrian	Syrian
Tanzania	Tanzanian	Swahili/English
Thailand	Thai	Thai
Turkey	Turkish	Turkish
the United States	American	English
Uruguay	Uruguayan	Spanish
Venezuela	Venezuelan	Spanish
Zaire	Zairian	French/Bantu

B Phonetic Symbols

Consonants

[p]	piano, apple
[t]	ten, can't
[k]	coffee, like
[b]	bank, cabbage
[d]	dinner, idea
[g]	good, drugstore
[f]	five, after
[v]	very, have
[θ]	thirsty, path
[ð]	the, mother
[s]	some, dress
[z]	zero, busy
[š]	shoe, information
[ž]	pleasure, measure
[č]	children, teach
[j]	juice, age
[l]	letter, mile
[r]	right, sorry
[m]	many, name
[n]	never, money
[ŋ]	key ring, sing
[w]	water, housework
[y]	year, million
[h]	hat, offhand

Vowels

[iy]	meet, tea
[i]	in, city
[ey]	waiter, great
[e]	hello, help
[æ]	ask, family
[ə]	appointment, but
[a]	father, hot
[uw]	you, boom
[u]	could, put
[ow]	home, go
[ɔ]	water, ball
[ay]	dime, night
[aw]	pound, house
[ɔy]	boy, join

C Some Common Irregular Verbs

Base Form	Present Tense	Past Tense	Present Participle	Past Participle
be	am, is, are	was, were	being	been
become	become, becomes	became	becoming	become
begin	begin, begins	began	beginning	begun
blow	blow, blows	blew	blowing	blown
break	break, breaks	broke	breaking	broken
bring	bring, brings	brought	bringing	brought
build	build, builds	built	building	built
buy	buy, buys	bought	buying	bought
catch	catch, catches	caught	catching	caught
come	come, comes	came	coming	come
cost	cost, costs	cost	costing	cost
do	do, does	did	doing	done
drink	drink, drinks	drank	drinking	drunk
eat	eat, eats	ate	eating	eaten
fall	fall, falls	fell	falling	fallen
feed	feed, feeds	fed	feeding	fed
feel	feel, feels	felt	feeling	felt
fight	fight, fights	fought	fighting	fought
find	find, finds	found	finding	found
fly	fly, flies	flew	flying	flown
forget	forget, forgets	forgot	forgetting	forgotten
freeze	freeze, freezes	froze	freezing	frozen
get	get, gets	got	getting	gotten (or got)
give	give, gives	gave	giving	given
go	go, goes	went	going	gone
grow	grow, grows	grew	growing	grown
have	have, has	had	having	had
hear	hear, hears	heard	hearing	heard
hide	hide, hides	hid	hiding	hidden
hit	hit, hits	hit	hitting	hit
hold	hold, holds	held	holding	held
hurt	hurt, hurts	hurt	hurting	hurt
keep	keep, keeps	kept	keeping	kept
lay	lay, lays	laid	laying	laid
leave	leave, leaves	left	leaving	left
lend	lend, lends	lent	lending	lent
let	let, lets	let	letting	let
lie (recline)	lie, lies	lay	lying	lain
lie (untruth)	lie, lies	lied	lying	lied
lose	lose, loses	lost	losing	lost
make	make, makes	made	making	made
mean	mean, means	meant	meaning	meant
meet	meet, meets	met	meeting	met
mistake	mistake, mistakes	mistook	mistaking	mistaken
overcome	overcome, overcomes	overcame	overcoming	overcome
pay	pay, pays	paid	paying	paid

Base Form	Present Tense	Past Tense	Present Participle	Past Participle
put	put, puts	put	putting	put
quit	quit, quits	quit (or quitted)	quitting	quit
read	read, reads	read (pr. *red*)	reading	read (*red*)
ride	ride, rides	rode	riding	ridden
ring	ring, rings	rang	ringing	rung
rise	rise, rises	rose	rising	risen
run	run, runs	ran	running	run
say	say, says	said	saying	said
see	see, sees	saw	seeing	seen
sell	sell, sells	sold	selling	sold
send	send, sends	sent	sending	sent
show	show, shows	showed	showing	shown
shrink	shrink, shrinks	shrank (or shrunk)	shrinking	shrunk (or shrunken)
shut	shut, shuts	shut	shutting	shut
sing	sing, sings	sang	singing	sung
sit	sit, sits	sat	sitting	sat
sleep	sleep, sleeps	slept	sleeping	slept
speak	speak, speaks	spoke	speaking	spoken
spend	spend, spends	spent	spending	spent
stand	stand, stands	stood	standing	stood
steal	steal, steals	stole	stealing	stolen
swim	swim, swims	swam	swimming	swum
take	take, takes	took	taking	taken
teach	teach, teaches	taught	teaching	taught
tell	tell, tells	told	telling	told
think	think, thinks	thought	thinking	thought
throw	throw, throws	threw	throwing	thrown
understand	understand, understands	understood	understanding	understood
wear	wear, wears	worn	wearing	worn
win	win, wins	won	winning	won
write	write, writes	wrote	writing	written

D Vocabulary

This list contains all the words in the end-of-unit vocabulary lists together with the number, in parentheses, of the unit in which each word first appeared. Parentheses are omitted for words specifically taught within the unit.

A
abound, (3)
absence, 1
accident, (6)
accomplish, (7)
act, 4
action, 4

actually, (8)
adjust, (1)
advance, 5
advancement, 5
advertise, 5
advertisement, 5
affect, 1

afford, 6
alert, (1)
already, (2)
amendment, (6)
amuse, 3
analogy, (4)
analyze, 8

appoint, (6)
appreciate, (3)
argue, (8)
arrest, 6
associate with, (8)
astronaut, (5)
athlete, (8)
attend, (9)
attendance, (9)
attention, (3)
attract, (8)
audience, (3)
autobiography, (7)
average, (2)
avoid, (3)

B
bachelor's degree, 5
basic, (7)
be in charge, (9)
be interested in, (3)
be out of sight, (9)
behavior, 6
belief, (7)
bilingual, (9)
bloom, 4
boring, (9)
brainstorm, (4)
break, (3), 9
budget, 2
built-in, (6)

C
can't stand, (3)
candidate, 5
capsule, (5)
career, (8)
category, (5)
census, (2)
central, 8
century, (2)
chain, (9)
change, 1
cheap, 3
chief, (8)
citizen, 8
combination, 4
combine, 4
come up (with), (2)
compare, (9)
competence, (8)
competent, 8

complain, 3
component, (7)
computer, (7)
concentration, (1)
confidential, (2)
confused, (9)
connect, 4
connection, (4)
contain, (4)
contest, (3)
contribution, 7
control, (7)
conversing, 7
convince, (3)
coordination, (1)
cope (with), 1
core, 7
corporation, (7)
count, (2)
courage, (5)
court case, (6)
court, (6)
crash, 5
creative, (4)
cue, 1
curious, (4)
cut, 2
cycle, (1)

D
danger, (6)
dare, (9)
data, 2
dealer, 7
decade, 2
decline, 2
defend, (6)
degree, (5)
dehydrated, 5
delight, 4
dense, 5
deny, (3)
depend on, (2)
depend, 6
depressed, 1
determine, (1)
devastate, (6)
device, (6)
digestible, 5
direction, (7)
discourage, (6)

disoriented, 9
dispute, (8)
dress, (5)
drowsy, 1
dumb, 3

E
eager, 8
earn, 3
economy, 2
efficient, (4)
effort, (5)
emergency, (5)
employment, (2)
end up, (3)
energetic, (1)
energy, (1)
engineer, (5)
enormous, 8
entertainment, (3)
entire, 7
environment, 8
evaluate, (4)
excellent, (5)
executive, (8)
exotic, 8
experience, 5
experiment, 1
expert, 4
explode, (5)
explore, 8
explorer, (8)
express, (7)

F
facility, (2)
fad, (3)
fair, (6)
familiar, (8)
famous, (8)
faraway, (8)
figure, 2
fill out, 2
finding, 8
findings, (1)
fit, (5)
fix, (5)
float, (5)
fool, (9)
frequently, 1
fresh, (9)
funeral, (6)

G
genius, (1)
gentle, 5
get rid of, (4)
get something, (9)
get tired of, (3)
get up, (9)
give up, 6
glance, (9)
go crazy, (3)
go on (to), (7)
go out of business, (2)
go straight, (9)
go-ahead, (6)
goal, (6), 8
graduate, 5
guilty, 6

H
happen, 4
head for, (3)
hero, 8
hesitate, 7
highly, (7), 8
hire, (2)
hoarse, 7
honor, 8
household, (2)
humorous, (4)

I
identity, (8)
imagine, (4)
immediately, (7)
immigrant, (2)
improve, 4
in fact, (8)
include, (2)
income, (2)
individual, (2)
inefficient, 4
ineptitude, 8
influence, 8
innocent, 6
innovative, 9
instead, (8)
invent, 4
invention, 4
irritated, (1)
isolation, 1
I've been had!, (1)

J
jail, (6)
(jail) sentence, (6)
jeer, 9
judge, 4
judgment, 4
jury, (6)
just, (2)

K
keep in line, 9
keep track (of), 2

L
labor, (9)
landscape, (8)
launch, (5)
law, (6)
lawyer, (6)
lean, 3
license, (6)
lifestyle, (9)
lifetime, (2)
limit, 3
local, (2), 8
locate, (2)
look forward to, (3)
look up, 6

M
majority, (2)
make ends meet, 2
make sense, 4
mandatory, 6
mania, (3)
marathon, 3
marital status, (2)
market, (3), 7
master's degree, 5
maximum, (6)
measure, (1)
member, (6)
mess, (3)
method, (4)
minor, (8)
mistake, (4)
moisture, (5)
mood, (4)

N
nap, (1)
native, 8
natural, (1)
nearly, (2)

nervous, (7)

O
obey, (6)
offense, (6)
on the other hand, (8)
opposite, (5)
orbit, 5
order around, 9
organization, (6)
organize, (1)
original, (4), 8
outdo, 3
outlaw, (3)
overexert, 3
overexertion, (3)
own, (7)
owner, (7)

P
participate, 9
partner, 3
pay off, 2
peak, 1
penalty, (6)
percent, (1)
perfect, (3)
perform, 5
performance, 5
periodically, 7
persistence, (2)
persistent, 2
personal, (7)
personality, (8)
pet, (3)
petition, (6)
Ph.D., 5
physical, (5)
playful, (4)
pocket, (5)
point out, 6
politely, (2)
politician, (8)
popular, (3)
population, (2)
positive, (7)
practice, (9)
presence, (9)
prison, 6
problem, (4)
process, (8)
product, (4)

productive, (1)
program, (5)
proportion, 8
protect, (6)
psychologist, (8)
publicity, (6)

Q

qualification, 5
qualify, 5
questionnaire, (2)

R

reach, 7
real, (9)
realize, 1
recent, (5)
recently, (2)
recession, 3
record, (3)
recreation, 2
refer to, (8)
regret, (3)
related, (4)
relax, (4)
repeat, (1)
request, (1)
resident, (2)
responsibility, (7)
result, (9)
reveal, (1), 8
review, 6
rhythm, 1
rhythmic, (1)
rich, 8
ridiculous, 3
routine, 1
run away, 6
run into, 6
rush, (9)

S

sacrifice, (7)
satellite, 5
scary, (9)
schedule, (1)
search, (5)
sell like crazy, (3)
set an example, 9
settle down, 9
settler, 8
shape, (5)
sharply, 1

shout at, (9)
shuttle, 5
similar, (4)
similarity, (4)
simply, (7)
single, (9)
solution, (1), 4
solve, (4), 6
sore, 3
space, (3)
specialist, 5
specialize, 5
spit, 5
spotless, 9
stand at attention, (9)
stand over, 9
stare, 7
start over, (9)
stay, 2
steadily, 7
steal, (6)
stick, 4
sticky, 5
straight, 9
strict, (9)
struggle, 3
stuff, (3)
substitute, (4)
succeed, (9)
success, (1)
successful, (7)
suggestion, (8)
support, 7
sure, (5)
survive, 5
swallow, 5
swollen, (3)

T

take a nap, 1
take care (of), 9
task, 5
team, (5)
technique, (4)
temporary, 7
tenants, 7
think twice, (6)
thus, (8)
total, (2)
tough, (6)
treatment, (1)

trial, (6)
trouble, (3)
turn up, 7

U

uncertain, (9)
unemployment, (2)
unique, 8
upheaval, (7)

V

value, (7)
vary, 1
verdict, 6
version, (3)

W

waste, (1)
waste time, (1)
wealthy, (3)
weary, 3
weightlessness, (5)
welfare, (2)
while, 6
workaholic, 1

Y

yell, 3
yet, (2)

E Photo Credits

British Information Service, p. 2 *(top)*. The Bettmann Archive, 2 *(bottom)*, 3, 10 (both), 56, 57, 73, 86.
UPI/Bettmann, 4, 45 (center), 47, 72, 76 (right), 83, 108, 114. Courtesy of Apple Computer, Inc., 17, 152.
AP/Wide World Photos, 18, 19, 45 (right), 46, 47, 76 (left, center). Jim Kalett/Photo Researchers, 29.
Courtesy of the Ritz Carlton, Boston, Mass., 42 (top). Jeff Greenberg, 42 (bottom, both), 36, 69, 93 (all),
113 (top), 126. Courtesy of Vermont Travel Division, 55, 135, 164. Courtesy of National Aeronautics and
Space Administration, 77, 78, 88, 89 (both), 162. Frederick Lewis/Levick, 113 (bottom). Courtesy of the
Wang Center, 115 (top). Courtesy of Wang Laboratories, Inc., 115 (bottom). Courtesy of Maine State
Highway Commission, 131, 132. Courtesy of International Business Machines Corporation, 150 (left).
Courtesy of Nature's Classroom, Inc., 150 (center, right), 168. J. Paul MacDonald, 165.

F Text and Realia Credits

Page 95   MADD logo. Courtesy of Mothers Against Drunk Driving of Massachusetts
Page 123   "I See You Never" (excerpt). Reprinted by permission of Don Congdon Associates, Inc.
            Copyright © 1947, renewed 1974 by Ray Bradbury.
Page 152   "Book It!" logo. Courtesy of Book It!® National Reading Incentive Program.
Page 165   "Hardship, Help for First Time Offenders." Reprinted by permission from *The Christian
            Science Monitor*. ©1989, The Christian Science Publishing Society. All rights reserved.